LA FOCE

LA FOCE

A Garden and Landscape in Tuscany

BENEDETTA ORIGO • MORNA LIVINGSTON • LAURIE OLIN • JOHN DIXON HUNT

UNIVERSITY OF PENNSYLVANIA PRESS

PHILADELPHIA

PENN STUDIES IN LANDSCAPE ARCHITECTURE

JOHN DIXON HUNT

Series Editor

This series is dedicated to the study and promotion of a wide variety of approaches to landscape architecture, with special emphasis on connections between theory and practice. It includes monographs on key topics in history and theory, descriptions of projects by both established and rising designers, translations of major foreign-language texts, anthologies of theoretical and historical writings on classic issues, and critical writing by members of the profession of landscape architecture.

As part of the Penn Studies in Landscape Architecture, these visual and verbal approaches to La Foce inaugurate a sequence of volumes that will study individual works of twentieth-century landscape architecture. Through these it is hoped to explore the range and scope of specific examples of modern design, paying particular attention to the social and cultural contexts of each and to the relationship of one site to its surrounding territory. La Foce, Cecil Pinsent's masterpiece, is a splendid example with which to initiate such an inquiry.

Publication of this volume was assisted by grants from Friends of Festival in Terra di Siena, Inc.; Furthermore, the publication program of the J. M. Kaplan Fund; and the Samuel H. Kress Foundation

10 9 8 7 6 5 4 3 2 1

Published by
University of Pennsylvania Press
Philadelphia, Pennsylvania 19104-4011

Library of Congress Cataloging-in-Publication Data
La Foce : a garden and landscape in Tuscany / Benedetta Origo . . . [et al.].
    p. cm. — (Penn studies in landscape architecture)
    ISBN 0-8122-3593-2 (cloth)
    1. Villa La Foce (Chiusi, Italy). 2. Gardens—Italy—Chiusi. I. Origo, Benedetta. II. Series.
    SB466.I83 V555 2001
    712'.6'094558—dc21   2001027377

Printed in China

Contents

Preface

THIS IS A MULTIFACETED STUDY of the house, gardens, and estate of La Foce. It includes a historical essay and memoir by Benedetta Origo, the daughter of La Foce's creators (Antonio and Iris Origo), along with photographs, sketches, maps, and a critical analysis of the gardens created for the Origos in the 1920s and 1930s by Cecil Pinsent, an English architect and garden maker. The volume focuses primarily on these beautiful gardens; but they are seen by all the authors within the context of both the larger Tuscan topography and the wider landscape of geography and history.

La Foce, which means "the meeting place," lies at the confluence of two valleys, the Val d'Orcia and the Val di Chiana, in the southeast corner of the Province of Siena. Its land lies in four *comuni,* or townships: Chianciano, Pienza, Sarteano, and Montepulciano. Just before World War II, the estate of La Foce had reached 3,190 hectares (7,904 acres), comprising fifty-seven *case coloniche* (farms) run on the *mezzadria* (sharecropping) system. Notable buildings on the property, besides the farms, are La Foce—the villa and its gardens—where Benedetta Origo lives with her family; Castelluccio, a medieval castle, now mainly used for cultural events such as concerts and exhibitions; Chiarentana, once a fortified castle, now renovated and inhabited by Donata Origo; and the elementary school, the ambulatorio (clinic), Casa dei Bambini (children's home), and dopolavoro (workers' hall, now a trattoria), all built in the 1930s by Cecil Pinsent for Antonio and Iris Origo. In the 1970s, about one-third of the land was sold; the rest is now divided into two separate properties belonging to Benedetta and Donata.

Benedetta Origo   Laurie Olin

Morna Livingston   John Dixon Hunt

LA FOCE

BENEDETTA ORIGO

Between the Valley and the Mountain

THE MAKING OF LA FOCE

Preservo memorie non mie. —GIANCARLO PONTIGGIA

FIGURE 1. Val d'Orcia, with Monte Amiata in the background, in the late 1930s. (Photograph by Antonio Origo.)

TUSCANY, IN MOST PEOPLE'S MINDS, evokes appealing images of a centuries-old civilization, a place where nature itself appears tamed and enhanced by the presence of man. Images of Renaissance art and architecture, terraced hills neatly planted with vines and olive trees, monasteries and villas surrounded by woods and enclosed gardens all come to mind. Visitors travel along country roads that wind through prosperous villages with medieval centers, enticing shops, and well-dressed women. Fields are carefully tended, tomatoes and eggplants glow in the backyards, vineyards are heavy with grapes. Not a square meter is left unplanned. The legacy of Florence and its Medicean culture is a constant, reassuring presence.

In contrast, the Val d'Orcia comes as a shock to the stranger driving south from Chianciano, a watering-spa overlooking the fertile Val di Chiana, toward the Via Cassia, the ancient Rome-Florence road. The traveler suddenly reaches the top of a pass with a wide valley below: this is La Foce. Everything that can be seen from here appears conceived on a larger, wilder scale, very different from any other place in Tuscany. Even today, though no longer as bleak and infertile—"a lunar landscape, pale and inhuman"[1]—as it used to be when my parents first came to live here more than seventy years ago, the sheer breadth of the view is daunting. The wide and treeless valley is dominated on the horizon by the towering presence of Monte Amiata, a long-extinct volcano that rises in solitary majesty above the valley (figure 1). Low clay hillocks, the *crete senesi*, "as bare and colourless as elephants' backs, as mountains of the moon,"[2] on which little grows other than wild broom and prickly pear, ripple over the nearer ground. The Orcia River in the distance is a mere trickle of water in a wide stony bed. A winding road lined with small cypresses, their growth curbed by the wind and the hard, dry soil, zigzags up the hill to some abandoned farms. Under the clear blue sky, the basic colors are gray and brown and olive. The only villages in sight, over a vast expanse of ground, are far across the valley, on the greener slopes of Monte Amiata. Sparse farmhouses dot the landscape, a lonely medieval tower rises from the barren *crete* (figure 2), a couple of large water reservoirs testify to efforts at land reclamation. Only in spring, when the fields are covered with bright green wheat and the yellow broom lends color to the *crete*, does the valley appear more hospitable.

The traveler, sitting on the low wall overlooking the valley, is struck by the grandeur of the landscape, by a feeling of eternity and peace, of continuity, of the freedom that comes from great open spaces. Independent spirits and dissenters have felt at home here for centuries. The region has been a haven for heretics, saints, brigands, and partisans, who have found shelter in the woods and caves on the mountain, and followers in the villages. The Valdorciani are a proud, independent, and stubborn race; they have also learned to be suspicious of power. Romans, barbarians, Lombards, Carolingians, and Normans have descended upon them in turn. Feudal lords have fought over their land. The terrible wars between Guelfs and Ghibellines have destroyed their harvests and their homes.

Yet Tuscan civilization has left its mark here too. Several towns, abbeys, and castles, as well as paintings and frescoes, have survived and are recognized as some of Tuscany's most beautiful monuments. Many travelers come to see

Pienza, Pope Pius II's model city built between 1459 and 1462 by the Florentine architect Bernardo Rossellino, or San Quirico d'Orcia, where Frederick Barbarossa met Pope Hadrian IV to discuss peace and the fate of the heretic Arnaldo da Brescia. The great abbey of Sant'Antimo, founded by Charlemagne in the year 800 on his way to Rome, still stands in its lonely valley near Montalcino; and the region abounds in small, delightful museums full of local treasures.

THE MOUNTAIN

La Foce lies on a ridge of hills above the northern bank of the Orcia River, about 60 kilometers south of Siena. The highest point on the ridge is Monte Cetona, to the south. Here lies one of the oldest human settlements in Italy, Belverde—aptly named, as its prehistoric caves are buried beneath ilex woods and ivy. A charming Romanesque church, surrounded by ancient cypresses and the remains of its monastery, looks out toward the plains of Orvieto—a still unknown treasure in the 1930s when my mother took her old friend Bernard Berenson to see it on one of his early visits to La Foce.

On the opposite side of the valley, between La Foce and the sea, rises the bulk of Monte Amiata. The sun sets behind its dark shape in the evening, and it can still be seen at night, looming on the horizon, dimly lit by the stars. Its Fujiyama-like silhouette appeared in all my drawings as a child; and I loved being taken for walks in its cool beech woods or to pick chestnuts on its slopes.

Chestnuts, in fact, were about the only riches the Amiatini had, at least when I was a child. I remember my mother saying she had never seen such a grim, poverty-stricken place as Abbadia San Salvatore. Abbadia, a small town near the top of the mountain, had grown around one of the earliest and most powerful abbeys of the early Middle Ages, founded by a (probably legendary) monk who had obtained some land from the Lombard king Ratchis. Over the years the monastery had not only accumulated vast properties—legacies from rulers and lords in fear of damnation—but it had also collected a rich library. Unfortunately, by the time it was visited by Pope Pius II in the fifteenth century, the library had already been largely dispersed, though some of its codexes—including the precious Amiatina Bible, donated in 704 by Ceolfrid, abbot of Jarrow, to the Cathedra of St. Peter—eventually found their way to the Laurentian Library in Florence, where they can still be seen.

The mountain was much loved by Renaissance popes, who often went there in summer. In the sixteenth century, Marcello Cervini from Montepulciano—better known to us as Marcellus II, the pope for whom Palestrina wrote the beautiful *Missa Papae Marcelli*—had a villa-fortress built for himself at Vivo d'Orcia near the summit, where plentiful springs flow from a large underground natural reservoir (its water is now used for the whole town of Siena). The pope's heirs still live there.

Pope Pius II's description in his memoirs of his beloved mountain gives us a good idea of its beauty. The pope had found on Monte Amiata the large beams he needed for his palazzo in Pienza; and there he escaped from the heat one summer, bringing his court and cardinals with him.

> The mountain is covered in woods up to the highest peak, which is often hidden by clouds. Beeches grow at the top, then chestnuts, then oak or cork trees; on the lower slopes grow vines and other trees cultivated by human ingenuity, and tilled fields and

pastures. . . . Some of the oak trees have cavities that can hold twenty-five sheep. . . .

It was the month of July [1462] and the cherries were still not ripe up there. Pius lunched by a plentiful spring that gushed out of a nearby rock; then he heard the ambassadors' news and the petitions of the faithful. . . . If sweet shades and silver springs, green grass and smiling fields attract and inspire the poets, then it is here that they should stop in summer. . . . There are no serpents or dangerous wild beasts, no clouds of bothersome flies, one's face is not bitten by horseflies or midges, bedbugs do not spread their repulsive odor on your bed, mosquitoes do not whine in your ear; a great peace pervades the wood. Thorns and hedges do not scratch your feet, and there is so much space between the trees that their high branches can weave together and shade the grass below. The ground is covered with fragrant herbs and wild strawberries, and among them small streams of clear water whisper their eternal song. . . .

One day, while the pope was busy at his work, some dogs attacked a great deer who was lying there nearby, but he freed himself, kicking and flailing at his assailants with his horns, and in a flash was gone up the mountain.[3]

Abbadia San Salvatore had been a mining town (mercury) for a brief period of prosperity at the turn of the twentieth century. At that time it boasted a theater and an amateur orchestra; even the *barrocciai* (peddlers, drivers of mule carts) could recite entire verses of Tasso and Ariosto by heart. But in my time, soon after World War II, the mercury mines had closed, and the men were out of work. The theater was shut, and there was no heart any more for music and poetry. The children of Abbadia, it was said, roamed the dark streets at night, searching for their fathers in the taverns and bringing them home, drunk and violent.[4]

Tourism has now brought some relief from poverty: there is a ski resort on the mountain to which families from Siena, Perugia, and Arezzo come on weekends, and hiking trails have been marked in a ring all around it, providing beautiful cool walks in the woods. But it is unlikely today that a stag, if there are any left, will lie down beside you any more.

THE VALLEY

Monte Amiata is chiefly responsible for the peculiar inland climate of the Val d'Orcia, as the mountain prevents the mild sea breezes from reaching the val-

FIGURE 3. A view of the *crete*, or *biancane,* and the farm called Lucciola Bella. Except for the 1930s car, nothing much has changed to this day in this particular stretch of hills.

ley. Hard, dry summers, sudden hailstorms, and tearing winds—both the freezing northern *tramontana* and the hot dry *scirocco* from the south—do not make farming an easy task. Nor is it easy to turn the *crete* (or *biancane*)[5] into productive fields (figure 3). I remember my father laughingly telling us at lunch about an American visitor who had wanted to know what could grow on all that clay. "Bricks" was his ironic answer. "Well, build a factory up there, then!" the visitor had cried.

The valley's microclimate, the long dry spells broken by torrential rains, the lack of vegetation, all these causes have favored erosion, which is still progressing at the rate of about 3.6 centimeters per year. My parents worked hard to reclaim as much land as possible, leveling the clay hills—sometimes even blasting the rocks with dynamite—building dams and preventing further erosion. Today the *crete* are protected as part of the distinctive landscape of the Sienese countryside.

A recent study, carried out by the University of Florence[6] on La Foce land, has made the rather surprising discovery that most of the *crete* have only surfaced during the last 350 to 400 years, and that they are not due to a specific climactic period. In fact, in ancient times the valley's slopes were heavily wooded and the fields richly cultivated. In the fifteenth and early sixteenth centuries the Val d'Orcia was known as "il granaio di Siena" (Siena's granary); then the Guelfs and Ghibellines, in the bloody war between Florence and Siena, laid

FIGURES 4, 5. Two of the farmhouses on the estate, before their reconstruction. (Photographs by Antonio Origo.)

siege to the towns and destroyed the harvests, obliging the survivors and their families to escape to safer places. Destruction was so complete that many remote villages utterly disappeared. Soldiers complained that there was no booty worth taking, and to secure a single cow they had to travel for miles. Pienza itself was sacked fifteen times. Cosimo de' Medici, who by 1554 had Siena completely in his power, finally realized that at this rate the whole *contado* (territory) would be depopulated and started to bribe the fleeing population to return.[7]

But the valley never really recovered. And in the 1920s, when my parents came to live here, they found the farmers living in appalling poverty (figures 4, 5): "In the half-ruined farms the roofs leaked, the stairs were worn away, many windows were boarded up or stuffed with rags, the families (often consisting of more than twenty souls) were huddled together in dark, airless little rooms. In one of these, we found, in the same bed, an old man dying and a young woman giving birth. There was only the single school in the *fattoria*, and in many cases the distances were so great and the tracks so bad in winter, that only a few children could attend regularly."[8]

The *contadini* (farmers), not surprisingly, were illiterate and superstitious. Their only social occasions were the village fairs, some of which were well known for miles around. San Quirico d'Orcia, for instance, a large and prosperous village that owed its growth to its position on the busy Via Cassia (the

Roman road that for centuries provided the main link with the northern provinces), had a great cattle market and fair on the feast of Saint Luke (18 October), to which all the smaller villages flocked.

Tales and traditions were handed on from generation to generation in the long dark evenings by the fire. Some of the centuries-old superstitious practices were still followed in my parents' time.

> Some were frankly pagan in origin. There are still both witch-doctors and witches in the villages across the valley, and to one of these, a few years ago, two of our workmen took the bristles of some of our swine, which the vet had not been able to cure of the swine-fever. The bristles were examined, a little powder was strewn over them, and some herbs were given, to be burnt in their sties—after which the pigs did recover. . . . Divining of the future, too, was done. . . . An old man specialized in foretelling, in winter, the weather for each month of the following year, by placing in twelve onion skins, named for each month of the year, little heaps of salt. These he would then carefully examine: the skins in which the salt had remained, represented the months of drought; those in which it had dissolved, those of rain.[9]

Some places were thought of as miracle-working, too. Not far from La Foce there is a cliff cave (practically inaccessible today, owing to a landslide) called *poccie lattaie* (milky udders), where stalactites, looking remarkably like breasts, hang from the roof, gently dripping. It used to be the site of an Etruscan fertility cult (stone tools were found there, and a kind of font, shaped like a half-moon). It was still visited in my time by country women who were afraid of losing their milk.

Most of the local superstitions are now forgotten. Only when the need is dire are they sometimes—and rather shamefacedly—resuscitated. When my eldest daughter was married, we had planned to have a garden party (you can practically always count on the weather being, if anything, *too* hot and dry in July); but that year it had rained every day. The evening before the wedding, the highly literate son of an ex-laborer came to me and said, "Of course this is only a local superstition, but it can't do any harm to try! Let's put four brooms at the corners of the lawn and leave them there all night." The next morning dawned bright and sunny.

Monte Amiata's volcanic nature has provided the region with hot, mainly sulfuric, springs: Bagni di San Filippo halfway up the mountain, San Casciano dei Bagni near Radicofani, Chianciano near La Foce, and Bagno Vignoni all still offer their own special cures. Chianciano water, for instance, is supposed to be good for the liver: Horace had come here, on the advice of Augustus's doctor, Antonio Musa. San Filippo's waters are sulfurous and smelly, but the place, rather damply hidden in a fold of the Amiata, has a certain melancholy charm. San Casciano is undergoing an extensive face-lift these days, with the complete renovation of its baths.

Bagno Vignoni is the most interesting, though, with its vast medieval *piscina* (pool) in the center of the old square, where hot springs bubble up as though they came straight from Hades and envelop the tiny village with mist on cold winter nights. Vignoni boasts a list of eminent visitors. Saint Catherine of Siena was sent here by her family, in the hope that she would meet a nice young suitor and forget her religious "obsession"; Pope Pius II stayed in Vignoni several days to cure his digestive ailments; Lorenzo de' Medici used the mud baths for his arthritis. Montaigne, forced to stop nearby after an unfortunate crossing of a stream (one of his horses had lain down in the water, thereby wetting all of Montaigne's belongings and especially all his books— "il fallut du temps pour les sécher," he wrote crossly), was understandably unenchanted by Vignoni, and describes it thus: "Il y a dans ce lieu une douzaine de petites maisons peu commodes et désagréables qui l'entourent, et le tout paraît fort pouilleux."[10]

When the calcareous waters sediment and harden, they gradually form the beautiful travertine that is still used all over this part of Tuscany. One particular quarry at Vignoni was set aside by Pius II to be used exclusively for the church at Pienza, to which he planned to bring the entire papal court. Blocks from this same quarry, however, were surreptitiously turned into beautiful fireplaces, door frames, or wells for other owners too, and can still be seen in some of the houses and villages around Pienza.

PEOPLE

Many remarkable people have taken refuge in the wilderness of this region. Saint Francis is supposed to have spent some time in the caves—probably once Etruscan tombs—in the hills above La Foce. A painting in an altarpiece by Sassetta shows him crossing the Val d'Orcia on his travels between Rieti and Siena a year before his death. Monte Amiata rises in the background, tidy fields crisscross the valley, olive trees dot the hills under the walls of prosperous towns and castles. Francis pledges his life to Poverty with a ring, while Chastity and Obedience look on and Saint Bernardino stands just behind him (figure 6).

Saint Bernardino, too, a stern and caustic but much-loved preacher, roamed this valley and the mountain for many years. He had spent his novitiate in a small monastery, Il Colombaio (now a complete ruin), on Monte Amiata. Later he traveled all over Italy, preaching wherever he could find a gathering of people—at wayside shrines, on the threshing floors of farms, in stables and barns—walking barefoot and capturing his audience's attention with dry jokes and personal comments. "I see two women sleeping beside each other, and each is the other's pillow. . . . Women, if you were spinning and went to sleep, you would break your thread. I have spun and now I shall begin to weave." He amused his listeners with nicknames he invented on the spur of the moment. A careless housewife became Madama Aruffola (shaggy head); a girl always looking out into the street he called Monna Finestraiuola (*finestra* means window); as for the young gallants "in a tunic, with a page's haircut and long slit hose," these, he said, were "full of cock-a-doodle-do."[11]

Another saint, Romualdo, founder of the Camaldolese order (a branch of the Benedictines), in 1015 built a hermitage, Eremo del Vivo, on Amiata land given to him by Emperor Henry I (son of Frederick Barbarossa). His order grew to great power between the thirteenth and fourteenth centuries. The name of Romualdo, unusual elsewhere, is still given to boys born on the mountain.

Not only saints and hermits flourished in this region. Ghino di Tacco was a famous bandit, a robber baron, whose story was told by Boccaccio.[12] Lord of Radicofani (a castle poised high above a lonely stretch of the Via Cassia),

FIGURE 6. Sassetta, *Mystical Marriage of Saint Francis with the Virtues* (Musée Condé, Chantilly; photo: Giraudon). Saint Francis, followed by Saint Bernardino da Siena, pledges his life to Poverty as he travels across the Val d'Orcia.

Ghino used to swoop down on travelers and rob them of their goods. One day he captured the abbot of Cluny as he was making his way to a watering-spa with his mules and riches. While subjecting the fat prelate to a diet for several days—thus curing his dyspepsia—Ghino passed long hours with him in philosophical discussion. Then he freed the abbot, who in gratitude gained him the pardon of the pope, Boniface VIII.

A rebel and visionary of a different kind, David Lazzaretti was a strange figure who gathered a large following and much renown in the second half of the nineteenth century. One of six sons of a poor *barrocciaio* from Arcidosso on the Amiata, he was much admired for his strength and his inventive but blasphemous language—until he had a holy vision that convinced him he was a descendant of the French kings, with a direct line to God. After spending some years in France, where he wrote many of his religious and inflammatory tracts (he preached equality among men and entertained politically subversive ideas), he returned to his mountain. Here he collected more than two thousand followers, completely fascinated by his charisma, who built for their *profeta* a church, a tower, and a hermitage. He was shot down ten years later, in 1878, while leading a great procession from his mountain hermitage in the name of God and social equality, by the *carabinieri* of Arcidosso. Adherents to his word still meet every year on the mountain and follow esoteric practices in his memory.[13]

THE ROAD

"In the beginning there was a road," as the historian Joseph Bédier observed. Politics, creeds, opinions, civilization, all must rely on available means of communication. In our case, the history of the road, or network of roads, called Via Francigena[14] (which merges in part with the older Via Cassia of Roman times) gives us a better understanding of the making of Europe, providing a comprehensive view of the early centuries of our era, from the barbaric invasions to the modern world—a history of power, commerce, religion, wars, crusades. The Via Francigena was the road that connected France and the northern countries to Rome. This allowed pilgrims to travel directly between

FIGURE 7. Spedaletto, a fortified hospice on the Via Francigena in the valley, in the early twentieth century (it is now restored, but looks much the same). (I thank the Gruppo Pientino for the loan of this photograph.)

the two greatest sanctuaries of Christianity—Santiago de Compostela in Spain and Saint Peter's in Rome—and eventually from Rome to the Sepulcher of Christ in Jerusalem.[15]

Very early records of pilgrims' travels have come down to us. The *Tavola Peutingeriana*,[16] for instance, points out both Christian and pagan temples to be found on the road; and the itinerary of Sigeric, archbishop of Canterbury (994 A.D.), mentions all the stops and resting places on the way to Rome. The *chansons de geste*, sung by troubadours traveling from one sanctuary to another, also celebrate the roads on which they spent most of their lives: in one of these, dedicated to one Oggeri from Denmark, we find a description of our particular Tuscan stretch.[17]

Fortified hospices grew up along the road, at a distance of approximately a day's travel, where pilgrims, *clerici vagantes* (wandering clerics), preachers, and merchants could find shelter and food (figure 7).[18] Duchess Mathilde of Canossa, also known as Matilde di Toscana—a powerful and devout woman, who was in close touch with Cluny and the patriarchate of Jerusalem—had many hospices built along the Via Francigena. She traveled along it herself from Lucca to Rome, when she joined Pope Urban II and his Franco-Norman-Flemish army at the start of their crusade (1096).

Pievi, the first Christian churches initially built in the wake of evangelists from Byzantium, provided spiritual comfort and communion for the pilgrims. They were baptismal churches, where dedicated and unmarried young men could also receive instruction from the older priests. They were the only places, besides the great abbeys, where the tradition of learning was carried on throughout the Dark Ages.

Taverns, providing solace of a different kind, were to be found at every crossroad, giving rise to the saying "qui multum peregrinantur, raro sacrificantur" (he who travels much seldom makes sacrifices). La Foce was one of these taverns, strategically placed at the crossing of two roads that had been used continuously for many centuries.[19] It was built in 1498 by the greatest Sienese landowner of the time, the Hospital of Santa Maria della Scala.

Centuries before the tavern was built, however, La Foce was the site of a prosperous Etruscan potentate who ran the many small farms that covered the countryside and controlled the roads, one of which connected the inland towns—especially that most powerful one of Chiusi—with the coast. There was a large necropolis on the hill opposite the settlement: hundreds of tombs from the seventh century B.C. to the second century A.D., still being excavated today, testify to the wealth of the population and the continuous traffic on the roads.[20] At Chianciano, less than four miles away, a sanctuary dedicated to the cult of Sillene[21] was discovered recently. A terra-cotta relief shows the goddess driving a two-horse chariot, one of the best examples of Hellenistic art in Etruria (now in the delightful new archaeological museum of Chianciano, together with other finds from La Foce). In the nineteenth century, excavations had already been extensively—and illegally—carried out in the Chiusi-Chianciano vicinity. Leone Mieli, whose family owned La Foce from 1837 to 1924, was a most determined collector of Etruscan antiquities. He dug all over his property, with notable success, and finally donated his finds to the commune of Siena in 1882.[22]

The Romans subsequently turned the road into a real thoroughfare that converged on the Via Cassia. They also transformed the agricultural organization of the region. Great new farms grew up beside the main roads, rich centers dedicated to the cultivation of cereals such as *farro* (spelt) or wheat, with "Pompeian" vineyards and olive orchards.[23]

Along these roads, alas, the great barbaric invasions also descended, pillaging and burning, bringing fear and poverty, destroying the landed properties created by the Romans, and burying almost every vestige of civilization. The first and most powerful of these invaders were the Lombards (*Longobardi*, so-called because of their long beards), who settled all over Tuscia, as Tuscany was then called, during the sixth century A.D. They adopted the Arian religion, causing local strife and conflict with Rome and indeed causing the papacy to turn to the Franks for help. The Lombard queen Theodolinda, however, started an anti-Arian party in Rome with the help of Pope Gregory the Great. Following in her footsteps, it became the fashion among Lombard kings and noblemen to found monasteries and abbeys, often with hospices for the pilgrims, to which they donated land and privileges "pro remedio animae" (to save their soul). They also gave a new boost to agriculture, especially the cultivation of olives and grapes; and the *mezzadria* (sharecropping) system, which was to last until well after World War II, probably owes its origins to the Lombard domination.[24]

The Lombards were eventually ousted by Charlemagne, as he swiftly made his way south to Rome to be crowned emperor. Near Montalcino, Charlemagne's army was stricken with the plague and many died. On this spot the king built a church, Sant'Antimo (figure 8), which later became the second great abbey of the region (the first being San Salvatore on Monte Amiata). The monastery was closed in the fifteenth century by Pope Pius II on account of the monks' dissolute habits. The church, in its Romanesque version, is still standing in the center of a lovely vale, now cared for by a small group of French Dominicans.

The feudal system owes its beginnings to Charlemagne, who distributed conquered lands among his vassals. Most of the castles and strongholds in Val d'Orcia were built during this time: Rocca di Tintinnano, Ripa, Redcoc (Radi-

FIGURE 8. The abbey of Sant'Antimo as it stands today.

cofani), among many others. Some of the lords grew extremely powerful and dominated vast tracts of land. The Aldobrandeschi, who were said to own more castles than there are days in the year, were probably the most feared in the region—not least by the early Republic of Siena, which tried several times to bring them to heel. By the beginning of the thirteenth century, many of these nobles had been forced into town and, probably out of boredom, had begun to form free companies, dealing in money (the Sienese were then the bankers of the Holy See) but also trading in all kinds of goods with England and France and the East. At this point it became urgent for Siena to ensure the safety of its roads, which were infested by bandits who would attack and plunder the merchant caravans, sometimes in gangs of thirty or forty men, and by robber barons who exacted heavy dues from anyone crossing their lands or bridges. However, it was only after many years and a series of bloody battles that all the castles of Val d'Orcia were finally subjugated by the republic.

CASTELLUCCIO

One of the most solid institutions of Siena, a strife-ridden city with litigious factions among its citizens, was the Spedale (hospital) of Santa Maria della Scala. The great hospital, where Saint Bernardino had tended the sick during the plague, was founded in the eleventh century. It contained a foundling hospital, a hospice for pilgrims, and a home for orphan girls (even providing a dowry for the girls when they married), as well as wards for the sick. This institution obtained its income chiefly from the lands it owned and the donations of wealthy Sienese families, among which, in the Val d'Orcia, were the estates of Castelluccio "Bifolci" (as it is called in a document of the twelfth century), Spedaletto, Chiarentana, and La Foce.

Castelluccio (literally, "little castle") lies on the summit of a hill on the La Foce estate. The precise date of its foundation is not known. It was probably built in the tenth or eleventh century, though it had certainly been the seat of an Etruscan acropolis centuries before that time. We do know that in the twelfth century it was in the hands of the Sinibaldi family, viscounts of Campiglia, and that in 1320 it was taken over by the *comunità* (commune) of

Monticchiello, a strong and fortified town, whose walls are still intact. Castelluccio contained a baptismal church, *plebes S. Iohannis de Villanova*, where Saint Bernardino once preached. Much later, under the reign of the dukes of Lorraine (eighteenth century), it became a parish church, taking the name of San Bernardino da Siena.

When I was a child, Mass was said here only on special feast days (on normal Sundays, we would walk through the woods to the cemetery chapel, much nearer our house), and on those occasions the church was always full.[25] On Palm Sunday the *contadini* would walk to church, some of them from very remote farms, carrying small olive branches to be blessed by the priest and then hung in the house for good luck; at Easter, it was eggs that got blessed, and we would eat them at lunch with wild *gallinella*, a delicious weed that grows in the fields. My mother would pedal away on the ancient harmonium behind the altar, accompanying the not always tuneful voices of children and adults right through the nineteenth-century "Gregorian" Mass that was considered appropriate at the time, with the occasional participation of our head *operaio* (laborer), husband of my mother's maid, and his trumpet, or of our local carpenter, Dante (who lived to well over ninety), and his violin, which sounded as if he had made it himself. I always wondered how people could concentrate on their souls during Holy Communion, with such a din going on.

The service in the cemetery chapel was much quieter and smaller (figures 9, 10). Practically the only attendance was provided by us Origos, a few farmers' families, and the children of the Casa dei Bambini (kindergarten) with their teacher (more about them later). The men did not enter the chapel. They all, including my father who towered above everyone else, stood outside under the portico, swinging on their heels, their hands behind their backs. On being asked why he did not sit with us, my father answered that if he stayed outside, he could keep his hat on—which seemed to me as good an answer as any. The Mass always ended with the children racing down the hill, then up another one, back to the La Foce garden, where we all—about ten or fifteen of us, usually—would play hide-and-seek until lunchtime.

The parish priest was an important figure in those times, who saw to the religious instruction of the schoolchildren, organized the May Day games, and often, being a young man himself, played football with the boys after catechism. The one I particularly remember was a man of unusual intelligence and goodness, Don Vasco Neri, who lived for many years at Castelluccio and was eventually transferred, when there was no longer need for a parish church here, to Monticchiello (about ten kilometers away; figure 11). In this small and completely communist village, he enrolled all the inhabitants, including women and children, in the writing, researching, and acting of a play every year, based on the village's history and its relation to modern times. A different theme was chosen each year: drought (a recurring problem in Val d'Orcia), old age, the war, village life.[26] He also organized Nativity plays in the village church, where there was a beautiful Lorenzetti Madonna, now in the museum at Pienza, often using medieval Italian texts provided by my mother.

To return to Castelluccio: at the end of the fourteenth century, the commune of Siena strengthened the castle's walls and donated it to the hospital. In this way Castelluccio became one of the hospital's *grancie fortificate* (fortified farms). Several *poderi* (dependent farms), a kiln (*fornace*), and eventually the Osteria La Foce were all run by the *granciere* who lived in the castle. One of these, clearly a staunch Ghibelline, took the law into his own hands one day, when the Medici pope Clement VII, on his way to confer with King Francis I in Marseilles, sent word that he would like to dine at Castelluccio. When the pope arrived, he found the castle doors firmly closed, and there was no way he could convince the *granciere* to open them. Clement, "with much inconvenience and hunger," had to drive on to Montepulciano.[27] When Siena, appalled by the possible consequences of such an action, sent ambassadors to apologize, Clement merely commented, "Le parole son femmine, ma i fatti son maschi" (words are feminine, but facts are male).

Castelluccio's fortunes, of course, were determined by the vagaries of the local wars, especially that most devastating one between Siena and Florence which, during the first half of the fifteenth century, emptied the countryside and drove the Sienese *contado* to ruin. On top of this, the plague of 1630, which had spared Siena but hit the country people hard, left the Val d'Orcia virtually uninhabited. The few farmers who survived were permanently in debt to the hospital, despite some "modern cultivations" (as they are described in a report by a Sienese inspector of the time), such as mulberry trees for the silk industry and new vineyards, which were eventually planted at the hospital's expense.

The hospital's domination, however, would not last much longer. The dukes of Lorraine, who in 1736 had succeeded the Medici as grand dukes of Tuscany and whose new, liberal-capitalistic policy included taking over church lands and redistributing them among the local nobility, put the Castelluccio property up for auction. It was bought by the Dei family from Chiusi, who later also acquired Chiarentana and La Foce—none of it prosperous land, to say the least. In fact, only a few years before, the last *granciere* of Castelluccio had warned the hospital about the speed at which erosion was advancing in the valley, owing to which one of the farms was even about to collapse.[28]

There was not much the Dei could do in these circumstances. The local situation was made worse by the difficulties that hit Tuscan agriculture in general at the beginning of the nineteenth century, caused in part by the free trade policy of the dukes of Lorraine, which had opened up the market to foreign competition (the price of wheat, in Florence, fell by as much as 50 percent). As a consequence, the poverty of the *mezzadri* became, if possible, even worse. The landowners, desperately trying to make ends meet, made even greater demands on the poor sharecroppers, obliging them to work longer hours and never investing in new techniques or equipment. An official visitor from Siena at that time describes the *mezzadri* as "full of apathy and ignorance . . . recalcitrant in the face of any betterment whatsoever." He specifically mentions those of "Castelluccio alle Foci" as "made to slave day and night with grave consequences to their health. I observed whole families become so exhausted by the month of August that they all fell ill, and the owner was obliged to send other laborers to store the wheat at his own expense, and take care of the ailing family as well."

In 1837 the estate, not surprisingly, went bankrupt. It was bought by Abramo Mieli, "a banker living in Rome," and his brother Tranquillo, together with their sons Angelo, Israele, Abramo, and Leone, who later divided the land of Castelluccio and La Foce/Chiarentana between them. Mieli must have seen this as an investment in line with the new agrarian policies of the grand duchy, which was trying to renew and rationalize techniques in order to bring a more competitive product on the international market. New capital employed in farming was much approved of; in fact, for some decades the system proved effective. It appears from the Mieli archives at La Foce that many agricultural changes were made during that period, especially by Leone Mieli (the same person who had a passion for Etruscan antiquities); many uncultivated fields around Castelluccio were turned into olive orchards and vineyards, some interspersed with mulberry trees, and reforestation was attempted on the hills. The La Foce/Chiarentana half of the estate, though, did not do so well: evaluations made in the 1920s show that only one-quarter of its fields were cultivated and that the owners were in debt to more than half of their *mezzadri*.

It is time here, I think, to say something about the institution of *mezzadria* in Tuscany, which lasted virtually unchanged until the 1950s. This is how my mother described it as it was in 1924, when she and my father acquired La Foce.

> It was a profit-sharing system by which the landowner . . . kept the farmhouses in repair, and supplied the capital for the purchase of half the livestock, seed, machinery etc., while the tenant . . . contributed, with the members of his family, the labor. When the crops were harvested, owner and tenant shared the profits in equal shares. In bad years . . . it was the owner who bore the losses and lent the tenant what was needed. . . .
>
> The origins of the *mezzadria* are easy to describe. After the breakup of the great feudal estates at the end of the twelfth century, most of the impoverished landowners moved to the rising trade cities (Pisa, Siena, Lucca, Florence) . . . while their starving serfs, whose fields and houses had been destroyed by a succession of petty wars, also fled to the towns, to find work and bread. . . . In a couple of generations they had saved

up a small hoard and since, sooner or later, the Tuscan has always been drawn back to the soil, their first instinct was to put it back into the land again. . . . As they could not afford to leave the town themselves, they set a laborer to work the land for them, drawing up a very simple profit-sharing contract, which gradually . . . came into universal use in Tuscany. . . . The serf of feudal days became a *mezzadro* or *colono*.[29]

A step up, one would think. Except that a bad, or simply a poor, landowner could be a disaster for everybody. In fact, in 1902 the *mezzadri* from Chiusi and Chianciano, followed later by the whole province of Siena, staged violent strikes, which eventually gained them better contractual conditions. But they were short-lived. The fascist regime, as soon as it came into power, imposed a "total reconfirmation of the fundamental principles of the classical *mezzadria*."[30]

This, then, was the age-old organization that my parents found in place when they bought the estates of La Foce (in 1924) and then Castelluccio (in 1934). It continued basically unchanged until the political struggles of the 1950s and 1960s, which eventually brought about the end of the *mezzadria*.

CHIARENTANA

When my parents came to the Val d'Orcia in 1924, Chiarentana was just one of the many farms dependent on La Foce, though it was certainly the largest, with more than twenty families and their livestock living around the big central courtyard (figure 12). Its history, however, goes much further back than La Foce's or even that of Castelluccio. Known in the early Middle Ages as Castello di Reggiano or Reiano, it included a baptismal church, the Pieve di Sant'Andrea. Emperor Otto I stopped here on his way to Rome in 962. Reiano also appears marked on a 1036 *Carta Amiatina* (a local map for the use of pilgrims). Chiarentana, in fact, was one of the many stops on this branch of the Via Francigena, a route that many pilgrims seem to have preferred in the earlier Christian centuries, and it certainly held a hospice as well as a church. In 1260 Chiarentana was donated by the Sienese republic to the Salimbeni family, in thanks for their role in the war against the Florentines.[31] This family of rich merchants, dealing mainly with the East, had acquired a large number of cas-

FIGURE 12. Chiarentana in the years before the war. The many haystacks bear testimony to the number of *contadino* families living there. (Photograph by Antonio Origo.)

tles in Val d'Orcia with the help of Siena, which was anxious to curtail the power of the far-reaching Aldobrandeschi family just across the river.

It was during the period of Salimbeni rule that the Chiarentana population drew up its remarkable Statute of laws (1314–16, privately printed by Leone Mieli in 1892).[32] This document specified punishments and rules for the population, dealing with every aspect of life, from the cutting of trees to fines for violence and adultery, and makes fascinating reading for anyone interested in the history and mores of those times.

The fortunes of Chiarentana followed those of its neighbors—a downhill story of war and devastation, poverty and degradation. My family restored it early on as one of the principal La Foce farms, but it always seemed a rather forbidding edifice to me, with high buttressed walls and a bare cobbled yard in which the north wind swirled unhindered (figures 13, 14). Morna Livingston's photographs bear testimony to the extraordinary transformation brought about in recent years by my sister Donata's imagination and hard work. Chiarentana has become her home, a warm, welcoming, cheerful place,

surrounded by a lovely garden full of lavender, rosemary, and roses that merges into the countryside.

LA FOCE

I would like to describe La Foce in the years before World War II as much as possible in the words of my parents. In 1936 my father read a paper at the Accademia dei Georgofili in Florence, in which he described La Foce and the "results of twelve years' work."[33] He typically began by disclaiming any particular competence in the agricultural field: "I am not a specialist, nor a scholar. I am simply a keen amateur farmer, who at a given point in his life—perhaps the most romantic one, coinciding as it did with marriage—felt . . . the eternal fascination of the country and decided to make it, and the people who cling to it for their livelihood, the main purpose of my life."

The description he gave of the valley reveals his love and dedication: "It is a vast and solemn landscape, where precipitous *crete* alternate with fertile oases. . . . The powerful spirit of a lost mythology hovers in the air above the valley, and an eternal sense of expectation reigns. . . . Neglect, destitution, and hopelessness seemed engraved on the men's faces and on the soil. We heard their call, we measured our strength and took our decision." The main points of his plan to develop the Val d'Orcia were:

1. set up an eight-year crop rotation
2. drain and build sustaining dams on the clay hills to prevent erosion
3. increase the arable land
4. rebuild the existing farms and the *fattoria* buildings and annexes
5. plant grapevines and olive trees
6. build new roads
7. build new farms
8. increase the livestock and create more pastures
9. suspend the cutting down of woods
10. increase facilities for education and medical care.

My mother points out in her autobiography that "the programme was a sound one, but its execution was slowed down not only by lack of experience, but of capital. Every penny we had, had been spent on the purchase of the estate."[34]

Even so, a great deal did in fact get done. By 1936, crop rotation was completely established on ten of the farms, and the wheat production had increased its yield; more arable land had been created by arresting erosion and extirpating rocks and boulders (figures 15, 16); the reconstruction of many crumbling farmhouses was under way, and the central *fattoria* buildings—granaries, olive oil mill, warehouses, garages for tractors—had been rebuilt; olive groves and vineyards had been planted on the better slopes; roads now

FIGURES 15, 16. Building retaining dams to prevent erosion and blasting the rocks with dynamite.

FIGURE 17. Long-horned *maremmani* oxen reaping wheat. They all had names and were shouted at continuously while at work, with many blasphemous epithets—a typically Tuscan habit, which did not particularly indicate anger or frustration. (Photograph by Antonio Origo.)

connected each farm, and a few new farms had been made;[35] the woods, which had suffered greatly from overgrazing and overcutting, had "grown miraculously," thanks to an eight-year rest and a development plan drawn up by a specialist. The number of sheep had been greatly increased. Even the cattle had grown more numerous: all *maremmani* or *chianini* oxen, they were used for farm work or meat (figure 17).[36]

The cheese made from sheep's milk—pecorino—is now a well-known Sienese product, even though the only sheep farms today belong to Sardinian families who had emigrated to Tuscany in the 1950s and 1960s, when much of the countryside was being abandoned by the local farmers. Pecorino cheese is now produced in modern dairies and can be found, fresh or mature, at any time of year; but in my childhood it was homemade, and the quality could vary enormously from farm to farm, depending not only on the pasture but on the ability (*la mano*) of each *massaia* (housewife); and fresh pecorino, as well as ricotta and *ravaggiolo* (made with whey), was available only after the lambs had been weaned, in the late spring.

FIGURE 18. The founda-
tions for a new farm being
laid, with the old one in the
background. (Photograph
by Antonio Origo.)

All this imposing volume of work could not have been carried out by my
parents alone. In 1927 a landowners' association was founded in the valley, the
Consorzio per la Bonifica della Val d'Orcia, with my father as "president and
moving spirit."[37] This entitled the members to state subsidies (from 20 to 100
percent of the costs, according to their nature) toward improvements such as
roads (eighty-three kilometers had been built by 1936), farmhouses and agricultural buildings, dams, reforestation, schools, and hospitals.

La Foce was by far the largest estate in the southern Sienese region. After
my parents' acquisition of Castelluccio and its farms, on the death of the last
Mieli heir (1934), the property consisted of 57 *poderi* (farms), including the
newly built ones, in an area of 3,190 hectares (7,904 acres), of which 555
hectares were woods. Much of the consortium's work was planned by my father, and much of it—but by no means all—was carried out on La Foce land.
Those were the years when neighbors from other estates used to say, on a Sunday: "Let's go and see what the Origos are up to in Val d'Orcia."

Roads, of course, were a priority. The little zigzag road that winds its way

FIGURE 19. The horse Grigia and our buggy. My mother, wearing a hat, holds me in her lap, and my Swiss nanny Tatina sits beside us.

up the clay hills, seemingly to no purpose, was in fact an essential step for the reclamation of the *crete*. Many people today think that it was created merely as a piece of picturesque landscaping, after the Lorenzetti frescoes in Siena; but in fact it was built by the consortium and represented, for my parents and the farmers, a hard-won conquest of new productive land on which to build more farms and keep them linked to the central *fattoria* (figure 18).

There was so much work to be done. Even after the war, I remember we were still fording the stream at the bottom of the hill to reach Chianciano, our nearest village—and in the wet season, it could only be crossed in a cart with high wheels. We had a nice horse called Grigia at the time and a little buggy that even my mother could manage (she was famously unable to deal with horses—or cars, for that matter), with which we would take little jaunts around the country (figure 19).

Not all the experiments, even though they were carried out with enthusiasm and imagination, were successful. My parents would tell with amusement about the Angus sheep, for example, expensively imported from Scotland, which were to be crossed with the local breed and thus improve the quality of their wool. Unfortunately, they all succumbed to tick fever.

Probably the most valuable and the most lasting work my parents carried out in those years was the construction of schools and kindergartens all over the valley. Both were very much needed, as more than 90 percent of the population was illiterate. They also built a small clinic at La Foce, the Ambulatorio Gianni Origo (named after my brother, who died of tubercular meningitis in 1933 at the age of eight), with beds for emergencies or childbirth, and a little apartment for the resident nurse.

Schools and hospitals were very much my mother's field. Though she writes, "I would try to make friends with the women and children. . . . The women were polite—and wary. I did not know the right questions to ask; . . . I could not tell one cheese from another; I had no idea whether the baby had measles or chicken-pox, and on the only occasion on which I attempted to give an injection to an old woman with asthma, I broke the syringe,"[38] everybody remembers her humanity, kindness, and generosity. In fact, she has become something of a legend in the region—and it is the very women with whom she felt "shy" who have given life to it.

I shall not dwell at length on the work, the improvements, the construction, in short the development my parents carried out; these have been described in detail in my mother's books. But I quote the words of some of their friends and collaborators who knew La Foce long before the war, and before I was born. Here is a school inspector describing his visit in 1934: "The owner's wife [Iris Origo] . . . had a passion for flowers; one could say she gave the teachers practical lessons in botany, with great tact, bringing vases with flowers and seeds to school. . . . She would come once or twice a week, without warning, and would ask after each child and his life at home, while looking at their work, pleased with their progress." Also: "On the main road that runs through the valley . . . one may meet, in the early morning or at sundown, a strange vehicle full of children who cheerfully call out to the passers-by: they are the pupils from the Casa dei Bambini at La Foce, going to their lessons or returning home."

FIGURE 20. The covered carriage that brought the kindergarten children to school every day. The children are dressed up for the inauguration of the so-called Dopolavoro (community center), also designed by Cecil Pinsent, where farmers and laborers could meet in the evening. The long wing held a small theater, which was also used as a dance hall on feast days.

The smaller children from remote farms were indeed brought to the Casa dei Bambini (the La Foce kindergarten) in a covered carriage—an unheard-of innovation (figure 20). The older ones had to walk, however. Those who had been up since six o'clock, and had already done the farm chores before leaving for the long hike to school, were sometimes too exhausted to concentrate; and when they returned home they were often sent out again, to run after the sheep or feed the pigs. Another difficulty was their scanty clothing, their broken shoes or wooden clogs, so that in winter they would arrive frozen and unable to hold a pencil in their hands. The teacher Ida Torriti wrote in 1942:

> Even though everything is provided for, even though the children are given anything they might need, still in October it is necessary for me to go the rounds of all the farmhouses and prod and persuade parents to send their children to school. . . . Nor will [the children] talk to me in front of their mother. To all, I say "tomorrow, tomorrow, at school, you'll tell me so many things, won't you?" As I leave, the *massaia* will call to me from the window: "Miss, Miss, take a bunch of these ripe grapes with you!" It is their tribute, and they all remember it.[39]

BENEDETTA ORIGO

FIGURE 21. The main
façade of the house, before
the war.

HOUSE AND GARDEN

In the meantime, my parents were also building their own house and garden, with the help of their English architect and friend, Cecil Pinsent (figure 21).[40] The history of La Foce, as a house, is not imposing. As a hostel, it had been granted "exemption from all burdens, tolls, and duties, as specified in the contract between the *spedale* and the *comune* of Chianciano."[41] From the end of the eighteenth century to the early nineteenth, La Foce was inhabited by a *fattore* (overseer), as both the Dei and the Mieli families preferred to live in Castelluccio. It had therefore become very shabby by the time my parents arrived. This is what they found.

> The home itself was certainly not the beautiful villa I had hoped for, but merely a medium-sized country house of quite pleasant proportions, adorned by a loggia on the ground floor, with arches of red brick and a façade with windows framed in the

same material. A deep stone staircase led straight into a dark central room, lit only by red and blue panes of Victorian glass inserted in the doors. . . . There was a general aroma of must, dust, and decay. There was no garden . . . and of course no bathroom. . . . There was no electric light, central heating or telephone.[42]

During their honeymoon, Pinsent carried out some basic work in the house: a skylight in the central room that would become the dining room, a library and sitting room, fireplaces made of the local travertine stone, and a bathroom (though there was very little water). His work on the "inner garden" did not begin until two years later. So it is not surprising that in 1925 my mother could write to Colin Mackenzie, a friend who lived in Scotland but who often came to stay here:

> La Foce is rather suited to meditation about the Brontës at the moment, and the bitter cold and howling wind which have prevailed in the last week are worthy of Yorkshire. . . . I am now very busy planning the nursery [she was expecting her first child] and the garden for the summer. For the latter I have at last managed to get a treasure of a gardener, and although he can't make flowers spring out of a dust heap with the rapidity I should like, he can at least remove the tin cans! (17 March)

All the same, she was already planting roses. On 11 December, she writes again to Colin: "The roses you sent me arrived this morning, as if in answer to prayer. . . . I have been digging ditches in the garden all day—and just before dark, had the satisfaction of seeing the last one in its place." In 1926 (22 August) the garden was still not ready: "You [Colin] will find the garden in the same deplorable state as it was 12 months ago—except for the bottomless pit dug to contain the non-existent fountain."

But Pinsent must have worked like mad, because the next letter to Colin contains the news that "the garden is unrecognizable since you saw it. Half of the façade is already re-stuccoed, and the fountain is in place. I'm going to pave the paths, too, with travertine, so that we should have at least one refuge on muddy days" (26 October 1926). And on 19 May 1927: "The garden is really much improved by being paved, the fountain looks lovely—the roses are in full bloom—and the whole countryside is deliciously green and springy. Yesterday I went down to the valley to watch the first day's haymaking. The movement

of the scythe—the long row of workers rising and bending with the rising and fall of the scythe—the smell of the newly-cut clover—it was all very delightful."[43] How happy she sounds—and how young. She was not yet twenty-five.

Colin's future wife, Clodagh Meade, who was still a child at that time, loved visiting La Foce with her parents. Eileen, her mother, was my mother's closest English friend. Clodagh writes, in a recent letter to me, "Your mother and mine used to strike sparks off each other, they had so much to talk about— books they had read, poetry, lists of bulbs they were going to buy, endless family gossip. They created an enjoyable atmosphere of what-is-going-to-happen-next." Clodagh, like me, also remembers "the lovely peaceful sound of the fountain playing." There were, and in fact still are, no other sounds to be heard at night: only the fountain, and nightingales in the spring, and owls calling to each other from the wood.

By the time my sister and I were born, all the building had been completed, of course, including the garden (figures 22, 23). In my time, even during the war, everything was comfortable and well organized. The only minor hard-

FIGURE 24. The dining room, with the light streaming in from the skylight, and the "wall frescoes in a baroque setting," designed by Pinsent.

ship I can remember is that water was chronically scarce, especially before the reservoir for irrigating the garden was made; and my father was always careful about saving electricity, though more from an inborn dislike of waste than any actual need.

The house itself was a constant source of exploration and delight for us, especially the attics and the cupboards all around the balustrade above our dining room, where old clothes were (and still are) kept for dressing-up—though at night the house could be quite scary too, with its long corridors and the uncanny silence. Pinsent's penchant for steps, sometimes purely arbitrary, leading to rooms at different levels and creating odd niches here and there, has always delighted me (I have noticed this feature in several other houses that he built). And the sense of architectural space and light that comes from La Foce's wide halls, paved in dark *cotto* tiles outlined with slabs of rough travertine, is unusual and very pleasant. The central dining room, with its imaginative, delicate landscapes painted in eighteenth-century style and framed by loggia-like arches, and the high Venetian balustrade above them, all lit by a central skylight, is one of Pinsent's chefs d'oeuvre (figure 24). It provided a brilliant solution for what had been a dark and gloomy room, barely lit by red and blue stained-glass doors leading into some bedrooms. Pinsent's landscapes were actually carried out by a local *pittore decoratore,* who declared, so the story goes, that he could paint anything that was required, provided there were not many trees, as he had never been able to master the rendering of leaves. Unfortunately all of Pinsent's plans and drawings for the house and garden were lost during the war—just a few torn and charred pieces of paper were eventually found in a field, completely ruined.

Years ago, my mother told an American friend, Isobel Roberts, that she wanted a garden "in which to read and think." I was reminded of John Dixon Hunt's theory that places—gardens and houses and the way they interact—are often a mirror of their maker's personality. Certainly the garden at La Foce was born out of a personal need, a specific desire, and for a definite use. It is not difficult to imagine how the harsh climate and the superhuman quality of the Val d'Orcia made it essential for my mother to create a kind of haven for herself, with green grass and flowers and geometrical box hedges to give a sense of order to nature, a place where she could not only "read and think," but write her books and talk to her friends. She would often sit in the morning under the wisteria-covered pergola, writing letters or reading to her children, or teaching us poetry. At the end of the day, she and my father would usually take a little walk together to the end of the garden to watch the sun set over the valley and talk over the day's events.

It seems to me, too, that my parents' whole enterprise can be seen in the light of Hunt's theory. La Foce is certainly a mirror of their two—very strong—personalities. Their need to have an ultimate goal that would justify their own life, to leave their mark in this world, to pit their strength against in-

FIGURE 25. Country
dances on the lawn in front
of the *limonaia* for my chris-
tening, August 1940.

numerable odds—as well as their sense of adventure and the desire to help others—all this was felt, in different degrees, by both my parents and led to the making of La Foce. *Per aspera ad astra*—I can't remember what led my mother to explain this motto to me when I was still quite young, but it comes back to me now as a very apposite comment on both my parents' lives. It is as a whole that their creation, La Foce, must be seen. As my mother once said to me: "It is the *fattoria* and the land that make this house and garden possible. Taken by themselves, they would have no sense at all."

CHILDHOOD

All this peaceful and busy life was suddenly cut short when Italy joined the war. In 1941 my mother wrote to Bernard Berenson in Florence: "Separation of all kinds—from family, friends, books, talk, everything except ideas—does seem to be one of the worst of the many bad things that this time has brought us."[44]

When Italy joined the war in 1940 (the year I was born; figure 25), my

FIGURE 26. Our family in the day nursery, autumn 1943.

mother was working for the Red Cross in Rome much of the time. In 1943, when she found she was expecting another baby (my sister Donata) she decided to stay more at home. How La Foce and the Val d'Orcia were affected by the war, she has herself told in great and moving detail in *War in Val d'Orcia*. All the same, I would like to give some idea of what our life was like at that time (figure 26).

La Foce during the war years had become a completely self-contained little community, producing vegetables and fruit, milk and cheese, jam and honey, meat, oil, wine, wool, and even saffron from the wild yellow crocus. The *fattoria* was teeming with people and activity. At least twelve men and women would sit down to meals in the *fattoria* kitchen every day: not the *fattore* and his family—they had their own apartment—but the *fattoressa* (who was not the *fattore*'s wife; she made the bread twice a week for us all, cooked and cared for the men, and looked after the chickens, rabbits, and geese), two or three *sottofattori* (the overseer's assistants), the dairyman, and several workers and gamekeepers (at that time we still had a game reserve). On a couple of occasions, after the war, I was allowed to have lunch there. Somehow, *fattoria* food seemed much tastier than ours, and there was always a lot of joking and fun around the table (though I sensed that their speech would have been freer, and the teasing more earthy, had I not been around).

I was very young during the war years. Even so, I have many memories of the events of 1943–44 which suddenly shattered my happy little life, sheltered as I had been by my parents, my nanny, and all the routine that makes childhood a safe place. Children, like dogs, are extremely sensitive to the feelings of adults around them—anxiety, fear, joy, anger are almost palpable elements in the air. I particularly remember, for instance, my parents' carefully controlled excitement when they came in the evening to hear the BBC on the radio hidden in the nursery toy cupboard; the arrival at La Foce of several refugee children whose houses in Turin and Genoa had been bombed; the anxiety, boredom, and discomfort of spending days and nights cooped up in the cellar under the house when La Foce was taken over by the Germans as their headquarters and we were being shelled by the Allies; my fear of "the bangs," as I called the bombs; feeling upset when our dog, Gambolino, was left behind in the rush of our own evacuation from La Foce. (Several days after our return, he came back from the woods where he had been hiding—but he was deaf and jumpy, and I became frightened of him.) I can also remember in great detail, for a child not yet four, the "walk" to Montepulciano across the fields: being told that I could not hold my mother's hand as I was "one of the big girls," and what's more I would have to carry my own winter coat (it was a hot June day); lying flat in a ditch while airplanes droned above us, ready to strafe anything that moved; my father suddenly bending down to pick a lucky four-leaf clover and holding it up in triumph, my baby sister crowing happily on his shoulders; my screams at the discovery that I had been sitting on an ant heap, after long hours of walking and being brave, and finding this just too much to bear; the cry of "E' arrivata La Foce!" (La Foce has arrived!) that came from the town walls as our friends, the Bracci family, finally caught sight of our straggling group rounding the hill and the relief of being lifted up on a man's back for the final climb to Montepulciano and shelter.

One of the refugee children from Genoa, many years later, wrote a touching testimony of what life was like at La Foce during those years.

> The marchesa was chiefly concerned with our happiness, and tried to calm the choruses of tears that occurred frequently during the day, particularly in the early hours of the evening. It was enough for one of the little ones to start calling *mamma,* and all the others, big and small, would join in. . . . Among my favorite memories is one of her descending the steps to our house with her small daughter, followed by a maid carrying an enormous box . . . from which she draws out many wonderful and to us unimaginable toys. . . .
>
> During the war years the marchesa would keep us busy in the big salon at the villa with songs and simple folk dances—some in Italian, but also English, French, or German—or she would dramatize legends and fairy tales for us to act. Her own evening dresses, hats and turbans, dressing gowns, and silk shirts made up our costumes.
>
> At Christmas we would act Nativity plays to an audience of their friends and the people who worked in the *fattoria,* after which the party would really start. The candles were lit on an enormous Christmas tree—and suddenly we would hear a great banging on the door, and Father Christmas would arrive with a great sack over his shoulder, full of presents for us all. For many, many years, it was the marchese, with red velvet dressing gown, white beard and a cavernous voice, who played this part. None of us children ever recognized him. . . .
>
> As for the marchesa, I can say I have loved her with immense admiration, then as now—not for the food, clothes, a home, presents, schooling, a diploma which she did indeed give us, but for her natural, almost detached way of encouraging us, of giving us the feeling that we were "all her children, one great family," as she herself once wrote to me, long afterwards.[45]

The children (figure 27) were living in the Casa dei Bambini, very close to our own house. It had originally been built, by Pinsent, as a kindergarten near the school, and bedrooms for the little refugees were added during the war years. Later it became a home for "orphaned, abandoned, illegitimate or under-nourished children," or those convalescing from tuberculosis (my mother had also founded a sanatorium in Florence for tubercular children, being particularly sensitive to this illness after the death of her own child), and

later still, for children in need of an adoptive home, which my mother would
find with the collaboration of the International Social Service. "My intention
was to keep it small enough to be as much like a family and as little like an institution as possible. . . . [There were] twenty children, boys and girls, between
the ages of four and twelve."[46] These children were our constant playmates
during the holidays. We organized games of football or volleyball, cross-coun-
try fox and hounds and races, or we explored the *crete* and the woods. On our
return, Signorina Vera, the directress (the children called her Tata), would feed
us thick slices of bread and homemade grape jam.

The *crete* were a never-ending source of wonder. One could easily get lost
in their crevices, for one thing, and only a good sense of direction could get
you home. Their slopes were steep, and sometimes the only way out was to
follow, crouching low, the paths made by wild boar and porcupines. In summer, the heady scent of broom warmed by the sun was intoxicating. And there
were always shell fossils to collect, and tunnels made by small animals to peer

into, and wet clay with which to make bowls and plates to dry in the sun and paint. We would also walk miles to swim in the rainwater reservoirs created by my father to irrigate the fields in the valley, and he would mercifully come to pick us up in his car in time for lunch.

The house itself was a good place in which to grow up. Sometimes the sheer size of it was difficult for a child to manage. There was a long way to run, holding one's breath, from the great *salone* downstairs, where the Christmas plays were acted out, to the safety of our nursery; and there was always a nasty moment of shadow and deep silence before one reached the light switch in the balconied dining room. Our fears were not made any better by the ghost stories that my mother loved to tell—always at night, in the half-dark, with my sister and myself and any friend that might be staying with us at the time all huddled in the same bed, clutching each other with excitement and pleasure. Another game we loved was Sardines-in-the-dark-all-over-the-house (attics and back stairs excepted); and after supper there were often guessing games or charades. Grown-up guests would also play, with the children fairly distributed in the teams according to age and ability—a very good way of stimulating a child's brain and social behavior.

Another fascinating place was the *guardaroba*, the ironing room, with its mixed smell of hot damp linen and lavender and the maids' laughter and gossip (not always quite comprehensible to me). Later, when we would spend the winters in Rome, chiefly for us to go to school, the household laundry would always be sent back to La Foce to be washed by hand in the open-air fountain in the courtyard; a truck went up and down each week, trundling laundry, firewood, wine, oil, pecorino, and prosciutto.

In summer we always looked forward to going to the *trebbiatura* (threshing) with our father (not our mother, I expect she had had enough of all that in the early days). The blinding sun seen through a haze of chaff, the noise of the threshing machine, the dust in one's nose, the oxen, the rides on top of the hay cart, the cigarette smoked in secret behind a hayrick with the younger farmhands, the long tables set out in the shade with white tablecloths, the wonderful lunch with *tagliatelle,* roast fowl and pork, and lots of red wine, and

FIGURE 28. Reaping wheat in the valley, with the Orcia River in the background and Monte Amiata on the horizon.

finally the pleasure of returning to our cool home, shutters closed against the sun—they are unforgettable memories and seem to belong to another era (figures 28, 29, 30).

The chief problem in Val d'Orcia was the lack of water. The wells my father had dug, trying to find underground veins with the help of a *rabdomante*, or water-diviner, were not very successful. During the 1950s, my father decided to make a couple of artificial lakes to hoard the winter rains and irrigate some fields, thus increasing their produce. These lakes—the making of them, first, and later their use for swimming—provided endless activity and fun for us during the summer holidays. There was no pool at La Foce in those days; in fact, my father firmly refused ever to make one (figures 31, 32).

Looking back at the years after the war, I marvel at how much freedom we were allowed, to roam about at will in woods and fields. This was considered a safe place then, I suppose: farmers were still living on the land and their women would always welcome us, often with pressing offers of biscuits and *vin santo* (sweet wine, which we didn't like but couldn't refuse), our parents had a good idea of where we were, and we were supposed to be able to look

FIGURE 29. Bringing in the sheaves. I am on top of the cart with some friends, and another friend "helps" the farmer drive the tractor. (Photograph by Antonio Origo.)

FIGURE 30. The *trebbiatura* (threshing). The wheat is separated from the stalks by a machine powered by a tractor. The sacks are weighed and a haystack is built. Many hands were needed for this work, so that all the farmers would go from one farm to the next, starting in the valley and ending with the highest on the hills, until all the wheat fields were reaped. (Photograph by Antonio Origo.)

FIGURE 31. The bulldozer, with Donata and myself participating, levels the ground for the construction of an artificial lake to be filled with rainwater for the irrigation of the fields in the valley (1954).

FIGURE 32. A couple of years later, the lake is full of water.

after ourselves. As long as we appeared home for lunch on time, with clean hands and brushed hair, my father very much encouraged independence. Indeed, the virtue I grew to consider above all others was courage: it was a masculine virtue, and therefore to be brave was the next best thing to turning into a boy myself. For the same reason, I would sometimes sleep outside in a tent rigged up in the garden, with my little sister: but while she would invariably ask me to take her home after a short and sleepless time, I would firmly return, scared stiff, to my lonely but exciting lair.

THE PAST THIRTY YEARS

This seemingly idyllic situation did not last long. Tough years were soon to come, filled with long and acrimonious workers' strikes, violence and class hatred, the breaking down of the *mezzadria,* ill-feeling, and disappointment. Stones were thrown at the house, insults and scowls replaced the smiles of welcome. Of these times, the 1950s and 1960s, my mother wrote: "We had become the Enemies of the People, the abusers of the poor. The church was no longer attended, and in the school the children's essays stated, a little puzzled, that now all the *padroni* had become 'bad.' . . . It was a painful, distressing period, in which all the evils—economic and social—that had been latent in the whole system of the *mezzadria* for so many centuries, came to the surface."[47]

It was during this period that my parents, under pressure from my mother's American family who feared that Italy would become communist, started thinking about selling La Foce. They looked at farms in Maryland and Virginia, and almost talked themselves into buying one. Back at La Foce, though, they both realized they could not abandon it. "We survived the war; surely we can survive this too," was how my mother put it later. Danger and difficulties, as during the war, seemed actually to bring them closer. My father told me once that the war had been their happiest period together—and though I was shocked at the time, I now know what he meant.

When my own children were young, in the 1970s, we were plagued by other fears. Those were the years of the Red Brigades and of kidnappings, some of which had been attributed to the so-called *Anonima sarda*. The Sardinian shepherds who had recently settled in the valley and taken over some of the abandoned farms were thought to be in league with the band. There were stories of bodies that had been cut up and fed to the pigs. It seemed as if La Foce would never find peace.

Things became so difficult that after my father's death in 1976, my sister and I decided to sell the whole property. Fortunately, as we see it now, the political situation and the opposition of the workers' unions made this impossible, and we eventually decided to sell about one-third of the land and divide the rest of the property between us. That third was bought in part by the Tuscan Region and put into the care of the Comunità Montana del Cetona (an offshoot of the Ministry of Forestry) and in part by a cooperative formed by former laborers and *mezzadri* from La Foce, with the financial backing of a state organization that subsidized small landowners turned farmers. The cooperative, sadly, went bankrupt through mismanagement and lack of experience, and the land was handed over to another, older cooperative of Sardinian shepherds, who are still there.

Those were the worst years: an angry period of transition. Though La Foce was only an echo of greater transformations worldwide, it was difficult at the time to see where they would all lead. Now the Val d'Orcia is a safe and friendly place again. Though agriculture here will never be easy, the European Economic Community has contributed in many ways to its maintenance, and a return to mere sheep farming and fallow fields has been avoided. Above all, the once-abandoned farmhouses have been put to a new and productive use as holiday homes, and the Val d'Orcia has recently become quite well known to lovers of Tuscany. What's more, the second generation of those *contadino* families who had gone to work in the towns is now coming back, sometimes just out of nostalgia, to show their children their old homes; but many have returned to live here, as a better and healthier place to bring up their families than our chaotic towns.

The admiration of others for our valley has made the Valdorciani proud of it themselves. In recent years, five communes in the valley (Pienza, Radicofani, Castiglione d'Orcia, San Quirico d'Orcia, and Montalcino) have agreed to develop a park together, the Parco Naturale, Artistico e Culturale della Val d'Orcia—no mean feat, as each *comune* wanted to impose its own leadership, and the contentious Tuscan spirit kept rearing up and making decisions difficult. With luck, the park will ensure that the valley is preserved in its present state and prevent the carrying out of such horrors as highways, factories, and new buildings, or the destruction of the *crete*, which, in spite of state protection, the small landowners still keep surreptitiously leveling in order to obtain more arable land.

There is also a chamber music festival here in July, the Incontri in Terra di Siena, based at Castelluccio and run by my son, Antonio Lysy, a professional cellist (figure 33). Musicians of all nationalities come to live in our restored farmhouses and share with an appreciative public the music they have worked on together. Other cultural activities—contemporary art exhibitions and courses in garden history and planning—take place here during the rest of the year. La Foce's garden is open to the public one day a week. Chiarentana provides a haven for many HIV-positive children from Rome and other towns, some of whom have never been in the country before.

FIGURE 33. Castelluccio's courtyard during one of the concerts of the Incontri in Terra di Siena festival. (Photograph by Zoltan Nagy.)

La Foce is now visited every year by thousands of people from all over the world, many with *War in Val d'Orcia* or *Images and Shadows* in their hands. "Sometimes," my mother wrote, "looking back upon all these changes and on the destruction or reversal of so many things that we have spent our lives in building up, we have been tempted to wonder whether all that time and energy was wasted, whether it has all been a mistake." In her heart, I am sure, she knew that though her world had changed, what she and my father had built together would last and be remembered by many generations (figure 34).

CECIL PINSENT'S WORK AT LA FOCE

1924   First alterations to villa

1924   Library, for use also as sitting room

1927   Inner garden with fountain

1928   Model of *casa colonica* (farmhouse)

1929   Entrance gateway, screen walks, and pillars

1929   Wall frescoes to dining room, landscapes in baroque setting (painted by Guido Agnelli from sketches by Pinsent)

1930   First extension of garden, box hedges and flowers

1931   Alteration and decoration of ground-floor sitting room

1931   Extension of *fattoria* forming courtyard

1931   Storage building for *fattoria*

1932   New suite of rooms for Origos on wing of villa, decorations

1933   Garage building

1933   *Ambulatorio* (first aid clinic, with beds)

1933   Cemetery and chapel

1933   Upper rose garden, new lemon house (*limonaia*), and lemon garden

1935   New altars and decoration of Castelluccio chapel

1935   Elementary school building

1935   Infants' school building

1936   *Dopolavoro* building for *contadini* and laborers

1936   Travertine paving of downstairs room

1939   Final extension of garden with travertine stairs, grotto, pond, and stone bench with statue

NOTES

1. Iris Origo, *Images and Shadows* (London, 1970; reprinted 1998), 200.
2. Iris Origo, *War in Val d'Orcia: An Italian War Diary, 1943–1944* (London, 1947; reprinted Boston, 1984), 7.
3. Pio II (Enea Silvio Piccolomini), *I Commentari,* ed. Giuseppe Bernetti (Siena, 1973), book IX, I, pp. 163–67.
4. Ildebrando Imberciadori, *Amiata e Maremma tra il IX e il XX secolo* (Parma, 1971).
5. Clay hillocks, called *biancane* (from *bianco,* white) because of a mineral, thenardite, that crops out and gives them a white shine.
6. Consiglio Nazionale per la Ricerca, Istituto per la genesi e l'ecologia del suolo, University of Florence.
7. One wonders what the valley would look like today if Pius II had been able to carry out his plan—"worthy of a pope who lived in peaceful times and was free from cares and wars," as he put it—of building a dam on the Orcia River and turning the whole upper valley into a lake.
8. I. Origo, *Images and Shadows,* 204.

9. Ibid., 210.

10. "In this place there are a dozen little houses around the baths, but they are disagreeable and uncomfortable, and it all seems very lice-ridden." Michel de Montaigne, *Journal de Voyage,* ed. Fausta Garavini (Paris, 1983), 340.

11. Iris Origo, *The World of San Bernardino* (New York, 1962).

12. Boccaccio, *Decamerone* (Day X, Novella no. 2).

13. Giacomo Barzellotti, *Monte Amiata e il suo Profeta* (Milan, 1910).

14. See Renato Stopani, *La Via Francigena: Una strada europea nell'Italia del Medioevo* (Florence, 1988; reprinted 1996).

15. To reach Jerusalem, pilgrims would travel on the Via Francigena to Rome, then take the Via Appia / Traiana to the ports of Puglia (Bari, Brindisi). After crossing the Adriatic, they would find the Via Egnatia, which took them all the way to Jerusalem.

16. A Roman itinerary of the fourth century A.D. that has come down to us in an early medieval version.

17. For further information on the early roads, see Alfredo Maroni, *Prime comunità cristiane e strade romane nei territori di Arezzo–Siena–Chiusi (dalle origini al secolo VIII)* (Siena, 1973).

18. Spedaletto, on the Via Francigena in the valley, is a perfectly preserved example of a fortified hospice.

19. Pre–Bronze Age tools carved out of oxidian, a hard black vulcanic material that is found only on the Lipari islands off Sicily, have recently been discovered near Chiarentana (Val d'Orcia), proving the existence of a commercial route here.

20. Recent excavations have discovered a Bronze Age (second millennium B.C.) settlement under the Etruscan tombs.

21. Or Selene, winged goddess of woods and nature, also mentioned in one of Pindar's odes.

22. Siena, Museo Archeologico Nazionale. For more information, see Giulio Paolucci, *Nuovi dati sulla Collezione Mieli del Museo Archeologico di Siena* (Florence, 1995). I thank Giulio Paolucci, director of the Chianciano Archaeological Museum, and the Etruscologist Sybille Haynes for their expert help and kindness to me in connection with this subject.

23. Spelt was much used in Roman cooking. Ovid also recommended its use as a cosmetic for women. In the "Pompeian" vineyards (so-called because they are depicted in the wall paintings of Pompeii), vines drape from tree to tree (either olive or fruit trees).

24. A contract drawn up in 736 at Agello in Val d'Orcia specifies the number of weeks a farmer had to work for his landowner, his share of the vineyard, and what gifts he was to make at Christmastime.

25. It is no longer a parish church and is mainly used for weddings and christenings, including those of our children and grandchildren.

26. Though Don Vasco died years ago, the plays are still performed in the village piazza every summer.

27. Arnaldo Verdiani Bandi, *I castelli della Val d'Orcia e la Repubblica di Siena* (Siena, 1926; reprinted 1973), 120.

28. I owe this and much of the following information to the doctoral thesis of Francesco Gazzabin, "La fattoria della Foce e Castelluccio in Val d'Orcia: Permanenza e trasformazione dall'età moderna alla contemporanea" (Università degli Studi di Firenze, 1997–98).

29. I. Origo, *Images and Shadows*, 213.

30. Giorgio Giorgetti, *Contadini e proprietari nell'Italia moderna* (Torino, 1974).

31. The war ended—for a while—with the terrible battle of Montaperti on the Arbia, in which the Florentines were killed in such great numbers that their blood "fece l'Arbia colorata in rosso" (turned the Arbia red). Dante mentions the battle in *The Divine Comedy, Inferno,* X and XXXII.

32. The statute has been recently reprinted: *In Val d'Orcia nel trecento: Lo statuto signorile di Chiarentana,* ed. Mahmoud Salem Elsheikh, presentation by Mario Ascheri, introduction by Alfio Cortonesi (Siena, 1990).

33. Antonio Origo, *Verso la bonifica integrale di un'azienda in Val d'Orcia* (Florence, 1937). The Accademia is a Florentine institution founded in 1753 during the rule of the dukes of Lorraine for the study and promotion of agriculture.

34. I. Origo, *Images and Shadows,* 218.

35. All the new buildings—school and kindergarten at La Foce, as well as the basic model for the farms—were designed by the architect Cecil Pinsent (see p. 51 for a list of his works at La Foce).

36. The gray, long-horned *maremmani* oxen are now practically extinct.

37. I. Origo, *Images and Shadows,* 219.

38. Ibid., 219.

39. The excerpts and information come from Antonio Mammana, "Scuole ed educazione in Val d'Orcia dal 1930 al 1945," doctoral thesis (Università degli Studi di Siena, 1989).

40. For dates, see p. 51 on Pinsent's work at La Foce.

41. From the *cabreo* (property map) of the Grancia del Castelluccio, 1763, in the archives of the Ospedale di S. Maria della Scala, now in the Archivio di Stato di Siena.

42. I. Origo, *Images and Shadows,* 203–4, which includes a more complete description of La Foce in the early years.

43. I am grateful to Caroline Moorehead, who has written a biography of my mother *Iris Origo, Marchesa of Val d'Orcia* (London: John Murray, 2000), for showing me these letters.

44. From Bernard Berenson's correspondence at Villa I Tatti (Harvard Center for Renaissance Studies).

45. Liberata Nardi, in Mammana, "Scuole ed educazione in Val d'Orcia."

46. I. Origo, *Images and Shadows,* 251.

47. Ibid., 247.

MORNA LIVINGSTON

Photographing La Foce

ONE HUNDRED PHOTOGRAPHS

I SAW LA FOCE FOR THE FIRST TIME in May 1997, when I came to document this unusual garden, which had just been opened to the public that year. Such twentieth-century gardens in Italy, and Cecil Pinsent's work in particular, had not been widely studied, except for some mention in articles and books. I knew La Foce only from an aerial photograph, the black-and-white photographs in Iris Origo's *Images and Shadows*, and three or four other photographs that people shared with me. The reality was infinitely richer than I imagined.

I brought three cameras: a Linhof 4 × 5 with Schneider lenses, a Hasselblad CM500 with Zeiss lenses, and a Leica M6. I used Provia 100 film by Fuji. With each camera I hoped to capture a different aspect of the garden. The Hasselblad gave the working format; the 4 × 5, with its deliberateness, corrected perspective and gave wide angles for certain views; and the Leica stayed in my hand in the rain and at the last hour of daylight, when I would walk through the garden to see what I had missed. I used Polaroids to study any particular problem.

I was allowed to work in the garden at all hours, thus I was free to discover it plant by plant. La Foce is a magnificent place to photograph on aesthetic grounds. It is neither as formal as most Italian gardens, nor as full of flowers as American or English gardens, but it is serene with a Tuscan rightness and changes constantly under the clear light. Near the house, the garden was planned as a series of distinct rooms, with glimpses of others beyond, but the rooms eventually give way to terraced fields on the hilly side of the property, and, further on, the terraces merge with the woods. On the open side is a view of Monte Amiata and the Val d'Orcia.

The plantings echo the quality of these rooms, becoming progressively less formal away from the house. Standard roses are planted in stone-edged beds near the house, climbers along the walls, and shrub and species roses on the far terraces. The transition from formal to informal was part of the original garden design. The garden's color is caught quite accurately on modern film, and the borders were a pleasure to photograph. The plant that ties La Foce together is wisteria. A white-flowering variety hangs like a curtain over the ramp to the wine cellar in the entrance garden, and a fragrant lavender wisteria grows on the private garden side along the upper terrace, curves around the hill, and continues toward the woods. The ribbon of twisted vines is solid flowers in April, velvet seedpods in June, yellow leaves in October, and gray lines in February. The weather in the garden seems to rise behind Monte Amiata in the distance. Between the mountain and La Foce's hill, a microclimate creates winds that keep the clouds in almost constant flux. Monte Amiata is the equivalent of Japan's Mount Fuji, with as many views as there are moments in the day.

There is a small tower near the main gate, where I first stayed. It overlooks the walled kitchen garden, now a plant nursery, and beyond that the Val d'Orcia. Later I stayed in the house. In photographing the house, I concentrated on details by Cecil Pinsent, such as the dining room with its Venetian gallery and trompe l'oeil frescoes on the wall and gallery ceiling, and on the travertine details of stonework in the interior. The material travertine is used to link the house and garden, as the wisteria ties the house to the woods.

Some things were hard to capture on film, while other parts of the garden fell into place at once. The garden is physically beautiful, but its character is stronger than mere surface beauty. This stems from the combination of cultivated and untamed plants, the changing topography of the various gardens arranged on the side of the hill, the juxtaposition of closed rooms and wide vistas, and the Tuscan light. Although the elements Pinsent used can be found in other gardens, photographs taken here show La Foce unmistakably, because of its underlying architecture. In this setting of clipped leaves and travertine stone, the plants appear like costumed actors on the scene—a tree of ripe pears, or *Salvia sclarea turkestanica* in a thunderstorm. The themes of the place, such as the rough Rapolano travertine and certain plants, change with the time of day, making it impossible to retake exterior photographs one day or even hours later and catch the same light.

Certain complementary relationships became clear only with time, such as the connection between the winding road to the farmhouse of San Bernardino and the series of rock gardens that rise to the statue of the Moor. I photographed some of these connections many times, but they were elusive. I grew almost superstitious about leaving La Foce, even briefly, afraid to break my bond with the place and miss some special light. Gradually, a series of images of the house, the garden, and the valley landscape took shape. Being there constantly, for a total of more than three months in different seasons, allowed me to see how the house and the garden were cared for, to hear the sound of the fountain and the intermittent noise of opening windows and shutters in the morning and closing them at night. Flowers and vegetables were brought in baskets from the garden to the house, hedges and trees were clipped twice a year, terra-cotta pots were moved from the *limonaia* on a dolly by six men and lifted onto plinths, a stone wall was rebuilt, the tall pines were pruned by gardeners swaying on ladders in the wind. Cool weather brought guests and family to a fire in the library; hot weather sent them to the pergola by the dolphin fountain. The garden did not exist in isolation; rather, it was part of the ongoing life of the Origo family then and now.

There are many sources of material on La Foce in the house, the library, and the *fattoria* office. There are Iris Origo's books, especially *War in Val d'Orcia* and *Images and Shadows*, in which she writes about life at La Foce, but also the *Merchant of Prato*, which gives a vibrant picture of Tuscan mercantile culture in the Middle Ages and makes clear its relationship to Tuscan *fattorie*. There are also garden notebooks that Iris kept, covering the years 1929–56 (with large gaps). The notebooks include lists of bulbs, seeds, plants, and nurseries, information about successes and failures of her plant choices, as well as a sketch plan of the beds in the lemon and rose gardens. The house also holds a large collection of books on the region's history, on the history of the *mezzadria* (sharecropping system), and on gardens, to which Benedetta Origo has added many volumes. There are recent aerial maps of the estate; a large hand-drawn *cabreo*, or estate map, dating from 1837; and a map painted on the wall of the main staircase dated 1941 that shows the many improvements that Antonio Origo made to La Foce's buildings, roads, and fields. Successive changes to La Foce, after 1941, were added to this map over the years. There is more information on the farm in Antonio's black-and-white photographic albums; he was always a keen photographer and a careful observer of the work in progress. The photographs, mounted under practical headings like "Taking Out Stones," document his comprehensive efforts to improve the estate.

At night, or when it rained, I read the books and studied the photographs in order to understand the valley. I became better acquainted with the four people who shaped this world: Antonio and Iris Origo; Cecil Pinsent, their architect; and Benedetta Origo, who owns the garden today. It became clear that the Origos lived the most creative part of their lives at La Foce and invested the landscape with their aspirations. Their attitude about what constitutes a worthwhile life, later inherited by their daughters, led Iris and Antonio to choose a path different from that of other wealthy landowners. Their life in the country, with its goal of remaking the run-down property into something productive, was a free choice on their part, not a necessity. They created a garden and transformed La Foce into a model of aesthetic beauty, modernizing an estate that had long ago been shaped by the social system of the *mezzadria*. It became clear that, in making a visual record, part of my task would be to capture these intentions, though the landscape is much changed today. When the Origos arrived in 1924, they found the landscape dry and eroded. In the 1920s and 1930s, development programs for southern Tuscany, such as making roads and putting in large drainage systems, were encouraged by Mussolini, and thus enlarged the scope of what the Origos could do on their own. The land changed under Antonio's direction, as miles of white roads (*strade bianche*) and stone-lined water channels were built.

The Origos had the advantage of an excellent landscape architect in Cecil Pinsent, who not only worked with them but was a lasting friend. Between 1923 and 1966, when he died, Pinsent had twenty-two commissions from the Origos, twice the number he had from any other client. When he worked on La Foce, he stayed as their guest for months at a time. He had known Iris from her girlhood and had designed a garden for her mother. His friendship with Iris continued and extended to Antonio when Iris married. The three were so close, they made a few trips together in the early years of Iris and Antonio's marriage in the mid-1920s. The strength of their long friendship lent a coherence to the design of La Foce, both in the garden and the close relationship of the garden to the landscape. During World War II, Pinsent went back England, but after 1945 he resumed extended visits to La Foce. The garden had reached completion by then, and it was a garden that was no longer feasible to build after the war, because of changes in the Val d'Orcia. Although Antonio concentrated more on the estate, and Iris, with Pinsent's help, more on the garden, they made decisions in consideration of one another. Pinsent's theory of design seems to have provided a kind of glue. Antonio's first photographs show bare land, scraped as if a glacier had passed over it. The three made the land come alive.

The herbaceous borders have been replanted with perennials to economize on the enormous amounts of labor expended in the past by Iris's more numerous gardeners—cutting hedges, watering, raking, bringing out garden furniture each day, planting from seed, making cuttings, bedding thousands of annuals, and, until the 1930s, caring for standard roses and many kinds of iris. Only traces of the older plantings remain, though the large clipped oaks in front of the house, the cypresses in front of the present entrance, the bay and box hedges, and the grotto near the dolphin fountain all remain. Some plants did not survive the changes in the labor force after the war, some did not survive the climate, and the bulbs in particular succumbed to the porcupines. Today La Foce has a comprehensive irrigation system extending as far as the woods, so that flowering shrubs can grow in the far reaches of the garden and plants in pots can bloom into the autumn along the stone walls and near the house.

Aside from the shift away from labor-intensive plantings, the most noticeable change that Benedetta Origo remembers from her childhood is the disappearance of the hedgerows from the landscape. Although today flowers, shrubs, brambles, and wild herbs do grow beside the less traveled *strade bianche* at La Foce, they are no longer trimmed to provide fruit, edible herbs, and sticks for fuel, as they were until after the war. The landscape of the Val d'Orcia, like the garden, changed in its details more than its structure, because of the departure of the *contadini*. The medieval complexity of Tuscan farming was erased after the war once the land had fewer people living on it.

I visited La Foce five times: one month during May and June 1997; a week in late February and March, five weeks in late May and June, and ten days in mid-October, all in 1998; and ten days in May and June 1999. Each trip gave me an opportunity to rethink the study prints, slides, and Polaroids. Each succeeding visit absorbed and surprised me. I was always discovering something I had not seen before; somehow the garden always managed to be new.

I hope my images have caught the triumph of texture, color, weather, and stone at La Foce; the estate as a testament to the extraordinary people who designed and built it; and the changing landscape as it accommodates both agritourism and agriculture. A photograph, of course, cannot capture the smell of the earth, a bay leaf, or a rose, nor catch the sound of water in the dolphin fountain. One can photograph the garden in the mist, but not the stone path to the woods on the nights before the wheat harvest, when the air is filled with fireflies, nor the double rainbow over the villa when it is pouring rain. To see the sun rise and be out in it until it sets, to watch gardeners trim the pines and move lemon pots—for all that, one must go to La Foce.

ONE HUNDRED PHOTOGRAPHS

1. LA FOCE THROUGH THE WISTERIA

The house seen from the upper garden, with the windows of three bedrooms. This is the old part of the house, originally built in the fifteenth century as an inn, where Antonio and Iris Origo lived before they added another wing. Cecil Pinsent partly redesigned its interior and opened a skylight in the ceiling to give light to the dining room.

2. THE HOUSE IN WINTER FROM THE PERGOLA

Only winter gives a clear view of the structure of the garden. This wide-angle view is taken from the wisteria arbor beside the rose garden, just before the path curves to the woods. The box hedges are trimmed in early spring and again in fall.

3. BOOKS IN THE LIBRARY OF LA FOCE

La Foce is full of books. These are in the library, but there are bookshelves on every floor of the house, arranged by subject—history, biography, letters, novels, travel, art, philosophy, poetry, even mysteries.

4. A RHOMBICUBOCTAHEDRON ON THE BALUSTRADE

Cecil Pinsent was interested in geometry. He placed one of these twenty-six-sided polyhedrons, also called a "square-spin," in the hall of the house; others mark the main entrance to the villa and the wall of the nearby kitchen garden. They catch the light in a characteristic way even at dusk or when it rains and change constantly in sunlight.

5. DINING ROOM

←As in many Tuscan villas, the dining room of La Foce has trompe l'oeil paintings, but here they take the place of windows. The paintings at La Foce are imaginary landscapes, not portraits of the Val d'Orcia. The room is furnished with painted chests and has a Venetian gallery above, whose ceiling, walls, and doors are also painted. The dining room gets daylight only from the skylight above.

6. GALLERY OVERLOOKING THE DINING ROOM

The floor is blue linoleum. The light is natural, including the light behind the open door, which comes from another small skylight. Pinsent had a penchant for adding small windows to let in light.

7. CLIPPED ENTRANCE TO THE GARDEN

This is the entrance to the garden from the courtyard in front of the oldest part of the building.

8. MONTE AMIATA IN EARLY MARCH

At daybreak, the colors of Monte Amiata's surface cover a wide spectrum from purple toward the summit to green in the valley.

9. MONTE AMIATA AND THE GARDEN AT SUNSET IN JUNE

← A view of the mountain, slightly to the left of the garden's main axis. The orange-red foliage is pomegranate.

10. THE ENTRANCE FROM THE FATTORIA

The side entrance leads into the main hall. This small garden is surrounded on two sides by the walls of the house and on the other two by clipped cypresses and a stone wall. The arched entrance to the garden is cut through the cypress. The small, clipped bay trees are hardy in Tuscany and remain in their box enclosures all year.

11. THE LIMONAIA

Citrus plants survive in northern Italian gardens only if they can winter over in greenhouses. In May they are moved by six men on a dolly from the *limonaia* to rest on marble plinths in the sun. In November they return to their home. On the hill seen in the distance there is an Etruscan necropolis.

12. THE GARDEN OUTSIDE THE SALONE AND THE GROTTO IN A MAY SHOWER

The garden near the house was the first to be designed, in 1927. It is only slightly higher than the old road that originally led to the inn.

13. THE DOLPHIN FOUNTAIN AT SUNSET

The central part of the fountain is antique (provenance unknown), and the surrounding basin was designed by Pinsent. The sound of the fountain makes this place the most soothing in the garden.

14. VIEW OF THE GARDEN FROM IRIS'S BEDROOM

This broad view in full summer shows the sequence of elements seen from the house: the garden with the bay grotto, the lemon garden, the wooded promontory on the tip of the hill, and Monte Amiata in the distance.

15. A ROW OF STONE VASES

Travertine vases line the garden wall, as seen from one of the guest rooms. The orange lichen shows how clean the air is in the Val d'Orcia, for lichen is sensitive to pollution.

16. A VASE AND CLEMATIS

Clematis armandii blooms in winter on the north wall of the garden, facing the sun.

17. VASES IN A STORM

← This door in the hedge marks the entrance to the lemon garden from the enclosed garden with the dolphin fountain.

18. VIEW FROM THE HOUSE AT SUNSET

At night the sun sets behind the bay hedges silhouetted against the sky.

← 19. WISTERIA ARBOR

20. WISTERIA PODS

In June the wisteria forms velvety seedpods. This vine is on the pergola in the garden with the dolphin fountain.

21. THE PERGOLA AND THE ROSE GARDEN

Roses are planted near the house and become twined with wisteria. On the left is the rose garden as it looks in early May. Where the pergola curves, the rose garden continues beside it, but only an aerial view would show the whole.

22. RIPE POMEGRANATES IN OCTOBER

23. ALLIUMS AND PEONIES IN THE ROSE GARDEN IN
EARLY SUMMER

24. THE LOWER GARDEN FROM ABOVE (OVERLEAF)

From the pergola above, one can see the different heights of successive enclosures—the hills, the garden wall, then the clipped hedges.

26. THE GARDEN FROM IRIS'S STUDY IN LATE
AFTERNOON

27. THE TRAVERTINE GROTTO IN THE LOWER
GARDEN, SEEN THROUGH THE WISTERIA

The grotto is made of travertine from Rapolano, near Siena. Iris Origo and Pinsent liked the roughness of this stone and used it all over the garden and in the house.

28. THE STATUE AND POOL IN THE LOWER GARDEN

The pool reflects the sculpture in the clear light of winter, when La Foce's palette is restricted to the colors of sky, grass, cypress, and travertine.

29. STATUE IN THE LOWER GARDEN

John Dixon Hunt recently identified this figure as one of a pair with the statue of the Moor at the top of the cypress walk (see no. 48). The two may have flanked the gate of an earlier garden in the area of Florence or Siena.

30. A PYRAMID IN THE LOWER GARDEN

Cecil Pinsent detailed all the stone in the garden, down to the last block. The pyramids prominently mark the balustrades of the lower garden, echoing the verticality of the cypresses that surround the entire space.

31. CAMPANULAS AND ROSES
← The campanulas thrive in the cracks of the travertine slabs. This curve has also encouraged the fragrant climbing rose Pierre de Ronsard.

32. BELVEDERE, CYPRESSES, AND MONTE AMIATA
From here, one can see the apselike opening of the belvedere from the end of the lemon garden, and beyond the wall the tops of *magnolia grandiflora* added after World War II.

33. URNS ON THE BELVEDERE

MORNA LIVINGSTON

34. THE BELVEDERE FROM ABOVE

35. LOOKING DOWN ON THE LEMON GARDEN

Only from above can you get a clear view of the formal rooms where lemon trees in large pots sit on stone plinths in the sun.

36. WISTERIA WITH LA FOCE'S SMALL CASA A TORRE
(HOUSE WITH TOWER) AND A HILL IN THE
DISTANCE

37. THE HILL ABOVE THE ROSE GARDEN WITH CLOUDS

The trees on the hill above the house are shaped by the wind. Cypresses were planted as windbreaks.

38. PERGOLA WITH A GLASS TABLE

This quiet part of the garden acts like a still pool in the series of garden spaces, rooms, stairs, and paths. Iris liked to write here in warm weather, sitting in a chaise longue.

39. GARDEN CHAIRS BY CECIL PINSENT

Pinsent's chairs are the traditional paint color for outdoor furniture, a green that was meant to blend with the landscape. This hue imitates an old form of green paint that used malachite as a pigment. This gives the green a haunting blue, rather than an olive cast.

40. TRAVERTINE BENCH WITH ROSES

All the stonework in the garden was designed by Pinsent. This bench faces the lawn in front of the *limonaia*. This lawn was used for gatherings in moments of celebration, including the birth of the Origos' daughter Benedetta. Now it has a swimming pool. The rose is Penelope.

41. FOUNTAIN IN THE LOWER GARDEN
The rusticated grotto is designed like a nymphaeum, with a fountain and tiered basin. The stone changes color with the light, from gray to gold.

42. THE GROTTO IN THE LOWER GARDEN
This was the final part of the garden designed by Cecil Pinsent; its construction is well documented by Antonio's photographs. It was completed just before the war in 1939.

43. DETAIL OF THE CLIPPED HEDGES IN THE LEMON GARDEN

44. VIEW OF WISTERIA IN BLOOM

These stairs lead to the rose garden beyond the wisteria arbor and to the cypress allée. The lemon pots are not yet on their plinths.

45. THE CYPRESS ALLÉE TO THE STATUE

← The travertine stairs give way to grass and travertine risers. Rapolano travertine is very porous, with small pockets that hold soil, roots, and moisture. Each step on this stair has a separate inventory of dwarf sedums and rock garden plants.

46. LOOKING ACROSS THE ROSE GARDEN

This is a view across the upper garden in June, when morning light rakes the stones of the path embedded in the hill.

48. THE MOOR

This statue marks the highest point of the garden. Its pair (no. 29) is at the bottom of the lower garden and carries tools, whereas the Moor holds a cornucopia of fruit and vegetables.

49. TRAVERTINE STEPS IN A STORM

This photograph was taken at the end of June.

50. WISTERIA AND THE MOON

Late in the afternoon, the wisteria turns a warm pink and later turns almost tan as the sun sets.

51. DWARF WATERLILIES IN A BASIN

There are two stone basins on the north wall of the garden, one of which now holds
miniature waterlilies.

52: VIEW OF THE LOWER GARDEN AND THE
LANDSCAPE

This is the most geometrical and "classical" part of the garden.

53. DETAIL OF A LOW WALL IN THE ROSE GARDEN

← Behind the geranium, a species rose on the grass terrace evokes the gardens of the Middle Ages.

54. THE LAVENDER BORDER

The rose garden has cultivated plantings of hybrid roses and climbers and is separated from the arbor by a lavender hedge.

55. DETAIL OF THE UPPER TERRACES

The wall divides the grass, which is freely planted with bulbs, fruit trees, and species roses, from the garden, where stone or box edges the beds.

56. VIEW OF THE TERRACES

This photograph was taken in October from the arbor in the rose garden. The wisteria pods are in silhouette.

57. BORDER WITH DAYLILIES

The borders at La Foce are influenced by the American and Irish gardens that Iris grew up in. Both sets of her grandparents had beautiful gardens. Italian gardens usually do not have many flowers, but La Foce is filled with them, and wild and cultivated flowers are arranged for the house in every season.

58. ROSA BANKSIAE ABOVE A BENCH AT SUNSET

This bench terminates the rose garden away from the house. Beyond the bench, cypresses shelter a similar bench, which looks out over the Val d'Orcia.

59. DETAIL OF A BORDER WITH MOSS AND PEONIES

The detail of the moss and flowering plants is typical of the planting of the flowering borders.

60. THE TERRACES IN AUTUMN

This path leads to the highest part of the garden, where it meets the principal path at the statue of the Moor. Each set of treads in the grass marks the level of a terrace that extends in a sweep toward the villa on one side and to the woods on the other.

61. BERGENIA AT SUNSET IN FEBRUARY

62. STEPS IN THE ROSE GARDEN
These lead from the rose garden to the grass terraces.

63. VIEW OF A PEAR TREE AND THE TERRACES

The garden on the terraces is reminiscent of medieval plantings, for there are white lilies, fruit trees like this pear, and grass scattered with wild orchids, violets, daisies, daffodils, calcicums, and crocus.

64. WISTERIA IN FLOWER

Among the plants, wisteria is the keynote of the garden, marking the entrance to the wine cellar on one side of the house and reemerging almost opposite on the other side. In the rose garden and beyond, it shades the path—a cord that ties the house to the woods.

65. THE WALL OF THE LEMON GARDEN

Clematis armandii covers the wall. Beneath the vase is a small basin of water.

66. THE WINDING ROAD SEEN THROUGH THE ARBOR

This curving road has become almost a symbol of the Tuscan countryside, and it can be seen from many places in the garden. It evokes similar roads in early Sienese paintings.

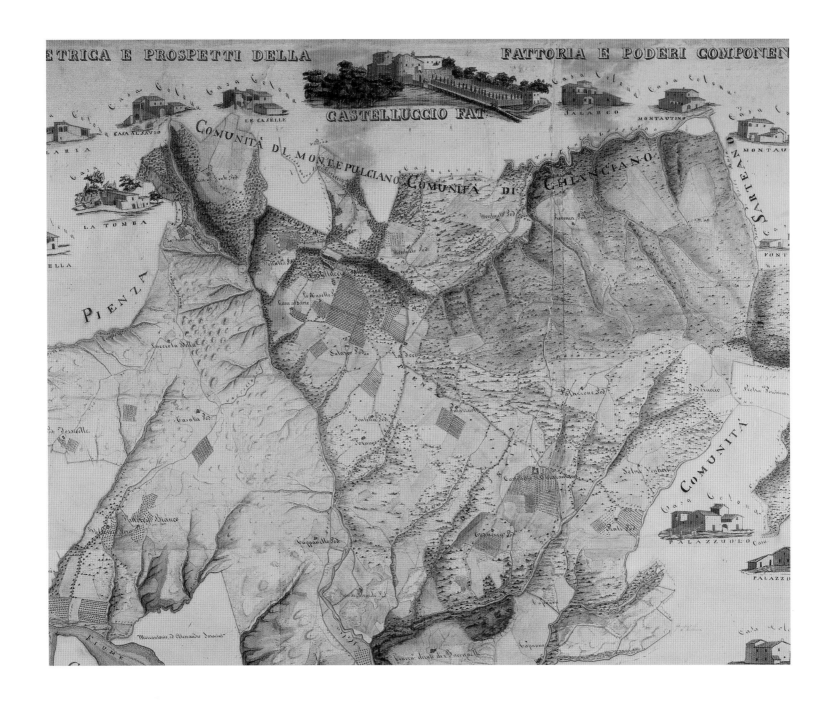

67. CABREO DETAIL

This hand-drawn *cabreo*, or estate map, of 1837 shows Castelluccio and La Foce. La Foce can be seen at the intersection of two roads below the U-shaped ridge at the top of the map, to the left of the center. All the farmhouses are identified by name. The square fields hold grapes or olives; the fields lined with furrows have grain or fodder.

MORNA LIVINGSTON

68. DETAIL OF THE 1941 MAP

A plan of the estate was painted on the staircase wall and modified as the years went by to show improvements to the land. Around the central map are the houses restored or newly built by the Origos, including the school, the clinic, and the cemetery.

69. DETAIL SEEN FROM THE UPPER BELVEDERE

← The landscape is visible from the semicircular terrace, which is the most open part along the path that leads to the woods.

70. WALL, CYPRESS, AND LANDSCAPE

It is interesting to compare this photograph of the mature garden with Antonio Origo's photographs of this garden under construction in 1939 (see Origo, figures 22, 23).

71. THE ARBOR IN SPRING

The path to the woods is shaded by an arbor. Here garden plants give way to plants of the
Tuscan landscape. Olives replace cherry trees, and grapevines replace wisteria.

72. THE ARBOR IN SUMMER

Near the woods, only one side of the path is edged in stone.

MORNA LIVINGSTON

73. DETAIL OF GRAPE LEAVES

74. THE ENTRANCE TO THE WINE CELLAR

Although La Foce no longer produces the good red and white wines it used to, it lies in the Chianti district known as Colli Senesi. Designated bottles of wine from grapes grown in the Sienese hills are marked with a cherub, or *putto*.

75. THE CHAPEL

After the death of Gianni Origo, the chapel and cemetery were built on a quiet road that leads to Chiarentana and Castiglioncello. Memorial masses are said here each year in June.

76. THE END OF THE ARBOR (OVERLEAF)

The stone paving under the arbor gives way to a grassy path in the woods. The path leads to the cemetery and chapel, designed by Cecil Pinsent, where Antonio, Iris, and their son, Gianni, are buried.

77. THE ENTRANCE TO THE FATTORIA

Though quiet today, this was the entrance to the central courtyard of the *fattoria* of La Foce, with doors to the olive presses, bread ovens, dairy, and winepresses. The opening in the far wall covers the fount.

78. CHIARENTANA

This composite building was a medieval walled *borgo* with a single gate. It had a charter by the fourteenth century and later housed several families farming *a mezzadria*. It belongs to Donata Origo and has a lovely modern garden. Today part of it is used for agritourism.

79. CASA DEI BAMBINI

Initially a kindergarten, the Casa dei Bambini housed refugee children during the war, then orphans until about 1956.

80. MONTAUTO WITH AN ALMOND TREE IN BLOOM

Montauto is one of the fifty-seven farmhouses, or *case coloniche*, that belonged to La Foce. This house was restored by Benedetta Origo and is used for agritourism.

81. THE KITCHEN GARDEN IN THE EARLY MORNING

The walled kitchen garden is laid out in four equal parts, like the garden of a monastery; today it is used as a plant nursery. Another kitchen garden has been planted on the other side of the house. The small trees are cypresses.

82. THE OLD STABLES

Above the stables are the living quarters, where *contadini* once stayed.

83. CASTELLUCCIO

← The previous owners, the Mielis, lived in this medieval castle. The present owner, Benedetta Origo, organizes concerts and art exhibitions here in the summer. As Iris described in *War in Val d'Orcia*, English prisoners were quartered here near the end of World War II.

84. CASTELLUCCIO FROM BELOW

Castelluccio faces a road that leads to Montepulciano and occupies a commanding position above the valley.

This door opens on the inner courtyard of the castle, in which chamber concerts are performed in summer.

86. THE CHAPEL AT CASTELLUCCIO

← The chapel, restored and enlarged by Cecil Pinsent, is still used for baptisms and occasional weddings in the Origo family. The baptismal font has a tile with their crest. The entrance is just inside the outer wall of Castelluccio.

87. CEILING FRESCO IN THE CHAPEL AT CASTELLUCCIO

88. THE ROAD TO SAN BERNARDINO

From many points in the garden, your eye is drawn to the striking form of this road, built after 1935 by Antonio Origo.

89. WHEAT FIELD AND BIANCANE

←The white clay mounds, called *crete senesi* or *biancane*, that lie beyond the wheat lend a particular character to southern Tuscany. They are now protected by the government as landmarks of the Sienese countryside.

90. BEEHIVES AND WHEAT

Beehives behind the *casa colonica* called La Fornace are rare in the valley today.

91. A LAKE

← This is the largest of the ponds created by Antonio Origo for the irrigation of the fields in the valley. It is fed by a stream, whose waters can be channeled into it, as well as by the winter rains.

92. OAK TREE ON THE ROAD TO CASTELLUCCIO

There are many references to "white roads," but the thick dust on the leaves along these roads gives a good idea of how they get that name.

93. PATH LEADING TO THE MOOR BY WAY OF THE
ROCK GARDEN

MORNA LIVINGSTON

94. LANDSCAPE: SALARCO

View taken from below Castelluccio looking across the valley.

95. LANDSCAPE WITH TORRE TARUGI

This tower is a reminder of how the Val d'Orcia was fought over during much of its history. It was a *casa colonica* under the Origos; now it is a privately owned farmhouse.

96. LANDSCAPE: FONTE AL GOZZO

The *casa colonica* is hidden behind the cypresses. The fields are gold with wheat about to be harvested.

97. FIELDS SEEN FROM THE GARDEN IN OCTOBER
← The purple-brown is rapeseed, a plant that tolerates dry conditions in summer.

98. THE FIELDS BENEATH CASTELLUCCIO WITH WHEAT AND AN OLIVE TREE
The landscape below Castelluccio has the classic Tuscan elements of *poggio* and *bosco*.
There are fields on the flatter land and woods on the slopes above.

99. VIEW FROM THE CASA DEI BAMBINI WITH WHEAT FIELDS AND BROOM

The Casa dei Bambini is the children's home built by the Origos. Wheat has been sown on the land reclaimed from the clay hills.

100. THE LANDSCAPE IN JUNE FROM THE PATH TO THE WOODS

Before a storm, or after a night of rain, the partial cloud cover lights the Val d'Orcia with spots of theatrical lighting against a darker ground. Depending on the speed of the clouds, these effects might last only a minute or two. The red patch is a field of poppies and the yellow broom is in full bloom.

LAURIE OLIN

Notes on Drawings of the Garden and
Landscape of La Foce

THIRTY-NINE DRAWINGS OF THE GARDEN AND LANDSCAPE OF LA FOCE

SITTING OUTDOORS SKETCHING and reflecting upon a scene and its details, which often reveal so much about how it came to be, is an activity and pleasure I have engaged in for the last forty years. In that time few places have given me as much pleasure or offered such a feast for the senses and mind in such a concentrated locus as La Foce, the Origo estate in Tuscany. The notes that follow were those made in a sketchbook during a weeklong stay at the villa in the summer of 1998. Some gaps have been filled in and a few additions made; extraneous and redundant comments were deleted. The fieldwork for the measured plan and cross sections was done the same week, as were most of the drawings and watercolors. A few additional sketches and comments were added on a subsequent visit in 1999.

29 June 98

Daybreak. Castiglioncello del Trinoro - Birds and bees warp
and buzz all about. above. below. Heard a cuckoo amid the rest.

1. THE ORCIA VALLEY SETTING

The still forested and rugged range leading to Monte Amiata is on the left, and the village of Castiglioncello del Trinoro is above on the right. The recent designation of large portions of this mountainous terrain, with its abundant wildlife, as an ecologically sensitive preserve, coupled with the numerous small settlements with off-the-beaten-track historic remains, churches, chapels, monasteries, and inns and superb regional food have led to a growing number of hikers and bicyclists, bird-watchers and photographers. Part of the region's salvation is the quality of many of the roads. Some are barely improved tracks, impassible at certain times, others steep and narrow gravel roads that barely accommodate two-way traffic.

2. CASTIGLIONCELLO DEL TRINORO

Like many other nearby hamlets and isolated villages, this small settlement once was part of the large landholdings of the religious order that held La Foce. Now, like most of the valley, it is independent. The many centuries of continuous landownership coupled with the difficulties of agriculture in this physiographic setting have led to slower incursions of modern life, imparting a quality to the region generally considered by many today as unspoiled, and leading to its selection and use as a movie location for historic settings.

13 July 1999 – Mt. Amiata from La Belvedere @ Castelluccio – La Foce.

14 July 1999   Castelluccio. approaching from La Foce up the gravel road through an oak forest

3. MONTE AMIATA (PRECEDING OVERLEAF)

As seen from the courtyard of one of the older farmsteads of La Foce adjacent to the ancient fortress of Castelluccio. A former granary is on the left. To the right are the former farmhouse and livestock quarters, now transformed into a caretaker's residence and two guest apartments. Referred to as the Belvedere, it has a magnificent view of this isolated volcanic peak. The highest summit south of the Arno in Tuscany, Monte Amiata looms above the valleys on either side of it, and, with its contributing flanks and great subterranean network of fissures, gives rise to many of the hot springs and ancient baths in the region.

4. CASTELLUCCIO

The first glimpse one receives upon coming up the oak-lined road from La Foce. Cecil Pinsent's austere chapel, used by the Origos, is found immediately inside the portal on the left.

5. CASTELLUCCIO

Reminders of earlier tempestuous days are found in the various coats of arms affixed to portions of the walls. This example is on the balcony over the entry gate. After many long years of weather and erosion, the lion above the shield looks more like Bert Lahr in *The Wizard of Oz* than a ferocious beast representing Florentine ascendancy over Siena, and the inscription on the lower plaque has been completely erased.

The coat of arms at Castelluccio is on the little balcony over the castle entry gate.

13 May 1999. The lion atop the shield/coat — more like Bert Lahr in the Wizard of Oz to me each time. Whatever had been inscribed on the lower plaque above the arch has been worn away, revealing next to nothing. This balcony — & the narrow bell tower — is one of the rare brick episodes in this castle's external appearance of brick masonry. In general it is (undressed or barely) dressed stone — rising dramatically & beautifully coursed and layed up to great heights — apparently 6 to 8 feet thick at the base.

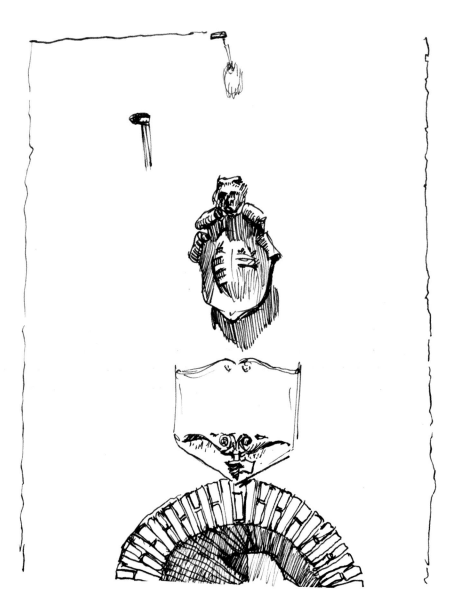

Castelluccio. 18 July 1999. Hot. dusty.

Perched high on an escarpment, the entry provides a pleasant sitting area beneath a large stone pine where visitors and locals come at the end of day to chat and look out into the deep space of the Val d'Orcia and across to Monte Amiata. The handsome brick gate on the left gives onto what is now the private garden of the Belvedere guest quarters.

7. NATURE RESURGENT (OVERLEAF)

In recent decades great strides have been made to conserve and replenish the ecological resources of the region that includes La Foce. The Provincia di Siena has recently posted "no hunting" signs along every road, and the estate office (*fattoria*) of La Foce boasts, through several framed certificates and awards of Antonio Origo from the 1930s to 1950s, of his achievements in forestry; the abundance of wild boar, deer, porcupine, rabbits, hares, eagles, hawks, owls, quail, doves, pheasants, songbirds, lizards, and frogs attests to their combined success. The control of the use of chemicals in commercial agriculture is attested to by the richness of native wildflowers and insects. In this sketch are seven of the ten species of butterfly that were foraging one of the lavender bushes in the dooryard one morning in July.

Some of the many butterflies on the lavender bushes at Castelluccio.

It seems that - with the exception of some spraying of fruit trees at particular times, that the Orcia valley and La Foce in particular are almost amusingly free of modern chemical pollution. This is easily attested to by the profusion of insects, plants, and birds that are so easily disrupted or eliminated by much chemical intrusion into the environment. I counted 10 species of butterfly on one lavender bush while sketching one morning, and the racket and constant presence of a large number and variety of songbirds, gamebirds, and raptors as well. Saw a hare one morning, and plenty of deer sign. While last year saw porcupines and knew of the _____ wild boars on the hills.

free scale.
Like everyone who has ever thought about such things it is still amazing to me that inside these little hand puzzle pieces is the genetic code to build a tree - Italian cypress cones @ La Foce.

Actual size of the small little oak leaves of the deciduous oaks in the forests of the Orcia valley.

PROVINCIA DI SIENNA
DI VIETO di CACCIA
Zona di Ripopolamento e Cattura

no hunting signs posted all around castelveccis and La Foce - as the government of the Provincia attempts to restore the richness of the ecology. Around here it's working well with wild boar, deer, porcupines, otters, eagles, owls, hawks and various quail, pheasants, etc.

Weather swirling around Mt. Amiata. 14 Jan 99. Belvedere @ Castelluccio, Tuscany

At times it disappears in the haze; at others it looms dark and ominous. Almost every day one or more clouds develop above or near it before moving off. Heavily forested with oak, pine, beech, and chestnut and replete with wildlife once more as in classical times, it has become a favorite destination for hiking and bird-watching.

The pen-and-ink sketch of the main entry of the villa from the Chianciano road depicts the original façade of the old inn originally built and operated by a Sienese hospital and its tenants. It is shown here nestled into the setting created by Cecil Pinsent in the brief period between 1929 and 1939. If not by Baldasare Peruzzi as some believe, the handsome and original façade of this building indicates a deep familiarity with his habits in the use of materials and the composition of a façade. Undoubtedly the three arches above the entry loggia were originally those of a second loggia that is now filled in with a bedroom suite and master bath. At the time, this view from the gate seemed a somewhat hopeless drawing, as everything was backlit and the spatial quality of the entry allée seemed lost to me. Later I learned to go here in the late afternoon when the sun falls upon the honey-colored stucco and warm brick pilasters and belt courses of the villa, and I made a watercolor (no. 11).

The building to the right in the sketch is an old stable from the time when the original *albergo* (inn) was in use. It is now a residence for a caretaker and family, with a cutting garden and nursery, now protected by several sleepy dogs, at the back.

In the front elevation as it is today, one still finds crests, insignia, and family coats of arms that testify to the sequence of ownership over time. Most relate to the hospital and its patrons who, the plaques explain, included the Piccolomini, Chigi, and Mieli families and a religious order represented by Saint Christopher and Mary enthroned in a cloud. The tiny aerial sketch is taken from a view of La Foce made in 1837 on a map of the region, now hanging in the hall of the villa. One can easily see the original plan of the old inn and the stables at the crossroad, also shown on this map.

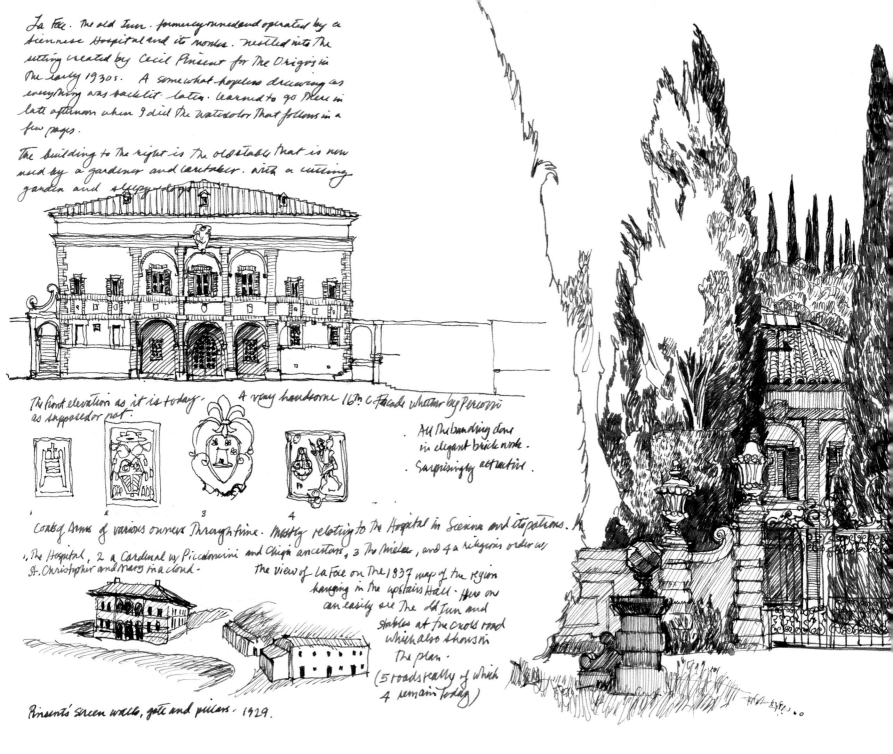

La Foce. The old Inn. formerly owned and operated by a
Siennese Hospital and its monks. nestled into the
setting created by Cecil Pinsent for the Origo's in
the early 1930s. A somewhat hopeless drawing as
everything was backlit. later. learned to go there in
late afternoon when I did the watercolor that follows in a
few pages.

The building to the right is the old stable that is now
used by a gardener and caretaker. with a cutting
garden and sleepy cat.

The front elevation as it is today. A very handsome 16th c. facade whether by Peruzzi
as supposed or not.

· All the building done
  in elegant brick work.
· Surprisingly attractive.

1   2   3   4

Coats of Arms of various owners through time. Mostly relating to the Hospital in Sienna and its patrons.
1. The Hospital, 2 a Cardinal w/ Piccolomini and Chigi ancestors, 3 the Mielar, and 4 a religious order w/
St. Christopher and Mary in a cloud.

the view of La Foce on the 1837 map of the region
hanging in the upstairs Hall. Here one
can easily see the old Inn and
stables at the cross road
which also shows in
the plan.
(5 roads really of which
4 remain today)

Pinsent's Screen walls, gate and pillars. 1929.

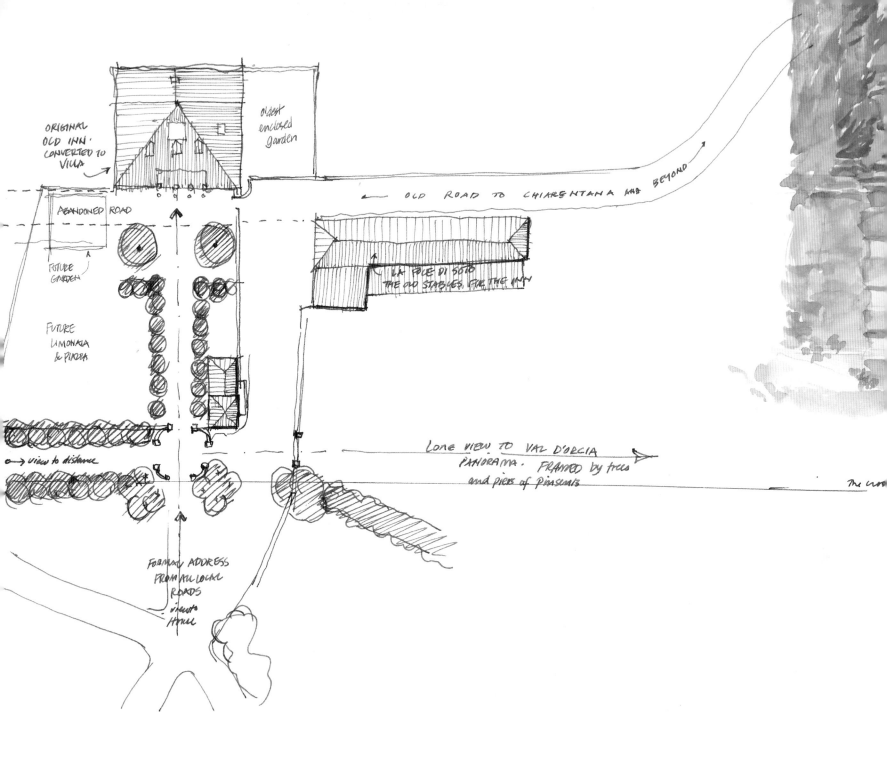

ORIGINAL
OLD INN
CONVERTED TO
VILLA

oldest
enclosed
garden

OLD ROAD TO CHIARENTANA AND BEYOND

ABANDONED ROAD

FUTURE
GARDEN

FUTURE
LIMONAIA
& PIAZZA

LA PILE DI SOTO
THE OLD STABLES FOR THE INN

view to distance

LONE VIEW TO VAL D'ORCIA
PANORAMA. FRAMED by trees
and piers of Pinascini

The cross

FORMAL ADDRESS
FROM ALL LOCAL
ROADS

view to
Hotel

main entry - near the old cross road. set up by Present and the Origos to present the Val D'Orcia
their property as the setting for the house and garden.

10. PINSENT'S DESIGN FOR THE ENTRY (PRECEDING)

Pinsent did far more than merely move the crossroad intersection, originally of three roads, but now only two: the Chianciano Terme to Val d'Orcia road and the Castelluccio to Castiglioncello del Trinoro (via Chiarentana) road, plus another now abandoned to the west. He also organized a sequence of spaces with trees and a handful of architectural elements—two sets of piers with urns, a low wall with notable geometric finials (rhombicuboctahedrons) to frame the view to the distant hills—so that the first sight a visitor is offered is that of the *crete senesi*, the barren clay hills of the greater region, and a sweeping view of the estate. Only then does one turn to look and pass through the gate and along the cypress allée to the villa. This foreground establishes a space for the villa and a transition from the outside world. It is a particularly effective sequence of domain and dominion.

11. ENTRY GATE AND ALLÉE

After beginning to make a habitable residence of the old *albergo*, Pinsent's first site design project was to move the ancient road away from the front of the villa to allow room for a gate and a respectable (if relatively short) entry drive and forecourt. The cypresses lining this drive, planted in 1929 and now more than seventy years old, provide privacy, a sense of age and authority, of patrimony.

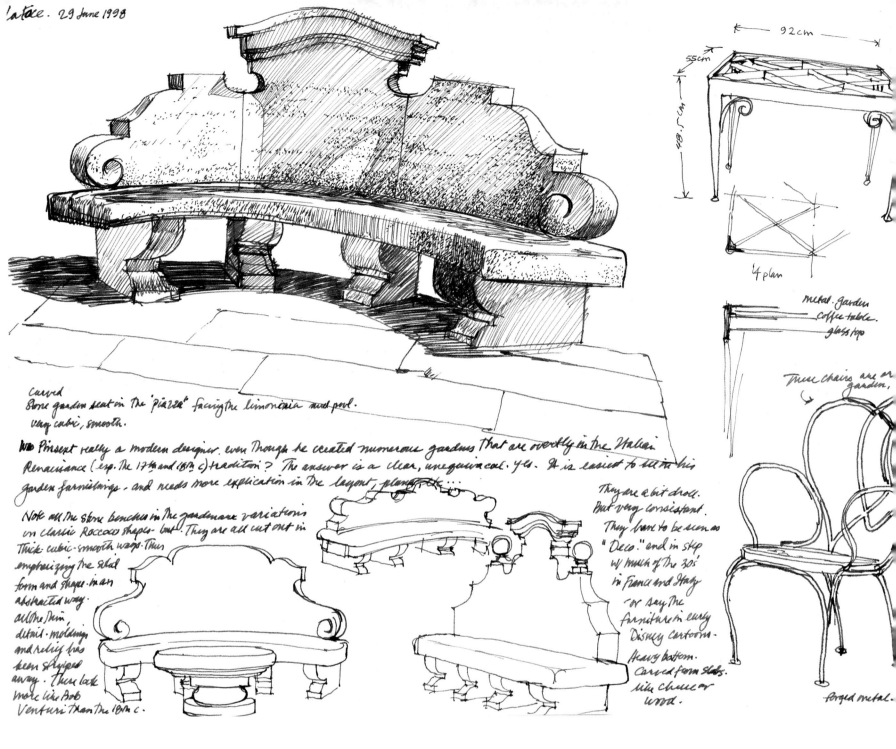

LaFace. 29 June 1998

92cm

55cm

48.5cm

4 plan

metal. garden
coffee table.
glass top

These chairs are in
garden,

Curved
Stone garden seat in the "piazza" facing the limonaia and pool.
very cubic, smooth.

Was Pinsent really a modern designer. even though he created numerous gardens that are overtly in the Italian
Renaissance (esp. the 17th and 18th c) tradition? The answer is a clear, unequivocal. yes. It is easiest to tell in his
garden furnishings - and needs more explication in the layout, plans, etc...

Note all the stone benches in the garden are variations
on classic Rococo shapes - but. They are all cut out in
thick. cubic-smooth ways. Thus
emphasizing the Silal
form and shape. in an
abstracted way.
all the trim,
detail. moldings
and relief has
been stripped
away. These look
more like Bob
Venturi than the 18th c.

They are a bit droll.
But very consistant.
They have to be seen as
"Deco" and in step
w/ much of the 30's
in France and Italy
or say the
furniture in early
Disney cartoons.

Heavy bottom.
Carved form Slabs.
like stone or
wood.

forged metal.

204

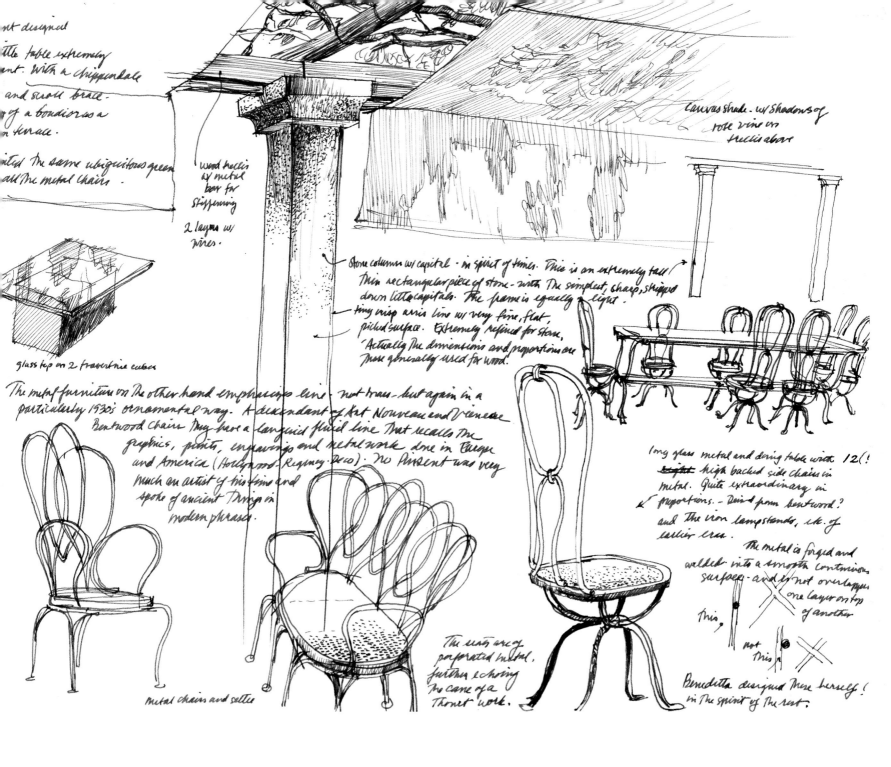

...nt designed

...tle table extremely
...nt. With a chippendale
...and scroll brace-
...of a boudoir as a
...n terrace.

...ted the same ubiquitous green
...all the metal chairs.

wood trellis
w/ metal
bar for
stiffening

2 layers w/
wires.

glass top on 2 travertine cubes

Canvas shade - w/ shadows of
rose vines on
trellis above

Stone column w/ capital - in spirit of times. This is an extremely tall
thin rectangular piece of stone - with the simplest, sharp, stripped
down little capitals. The frame is equally - light.
tiny crisp arris line w/ very fine, flat,
picked surface. Extremely refined for stone,
Actually the dimensions and proportions are
those generally used for wood.

The metal furniture on the other hand emphasizes line - not mass - but again in a
particularly 1930's ornamental way. A descendant of Art Nouveau and Viennese
Bentwood chairs they have a languid fluid line that recalls the
graphics, prints, engravings and metal work done in Europe
and America (Hollywood-Regency-Deco). No Pirsent was very
much an artist of his time and
spoke of ancient things in
modern phrases.

long glass metal and dining table with 12 (!)
~~eight~~ high backed side chairs in
metal. Quite extraordinary in
proportions. - Derived from bentwood?
and the iron lampstands, etc. of
earlier eras.

The metal is forged and
welded into a smooth continuous
surface - and is not overlapped
one layer on top
of another

this,

not
this

metal chairs and settee

The seats are of
perforated metal,
further echoing
the cane of a
Thonet work.

Benedetta designed these herself!
in the spirit of the rest.

205

12. FURNISHINGS AND MODERNITY (PRECEDING)

Although the first impression one gets at La Foce is of timelessness and that things must have been the way they are now for centuries, nearly everything is a twentieth-century invention, the majority of the environment set in motion in a brief ten-year period of intensive design and activity, followed by two generations of adjustment and fine-tuning. There is an air of continuity and tradition that is genuine. The minute one settles down to examine the elements, to stare at the fabric and details, one realizes that it is a modern world without pretension, which displays its modernity openly, with no apologies, while working within a clear and recognizable tradition of Italian gardens (not only of the Renaissance, but also of the seventeenth and eighteenth centuries) in many of their aspects as well as an agrarian land ethic. Nowhere is the modernity more obvious than in the garden furniture. With the exception of the tall-backed dining chairs and table (lower right) designed by Benedetta Origo herself a few years ago, all of these items—garden seats, tables, chairs, walls, and urns—were designed by Pinsent between 1930 and 1939.

All of the benches in the garden are variations on classic rococo shapes, but all are cut from travertine stone in thick, cubic, smooth ways that emphasize their solidity, form, and shape in an abstract way. All of the thin detail, moldings, and relief have been stripped away. They look more like Bob Venturi than the eighteenth century. They are a bit droll, but very considered. They tell us something about Pinsent's personality, wit, intelligence, and calculated artistry. They have to be seen as being infused with the spirit of "deco" and very much informed by fashion and in step with developments in France and Italy at the time, or with the furniture in the Disney cartoons of the 1930s—the heavy bottom, carved from slabs, like cheese or wood.

Even though carved by hand in quarries in western Tuscany, all of the architectural furnishings have been conceived and executed to resemble works resulting from machine-tool processes in their planar surfaces and geometric shapes. So, too, the metal garden chairs and settee, which, unlike the stone furniture, emphasize line not mass and, hand-made by local blacksmiths, do so in a particularly 1930s ornamental way. A descendant of art nouveau and Viennese bentwood, they have a languid, fluid line that recalls the graphics, prints, engravings, and metalwork done in Europe and America (think of Hollywood Regency) during the same period. Pinsent was very much an artist of his day and spoke of ancient things in modern phrases. The little metal and glass "deco" table I discovered in the villa, combining a Chinese Chippendale pattern with tapered neoclassical legs and bracket scrolls, seemed as worthy of a boudoir as the outdoors. When I asked Benedetta about it, she acknowledged that Pinsent had designed it originally for use in the garden.

After I had been drawing in the garden for several days, I realized something else that further confirmed Pinsent's modernity. Despite the evocation of traditional Italian garden design, replete with what appeared to be traditional (or traditionally inspired) garden seats with their curving backs and brackets, the balustrades, piers, urns, finials, and such ornament, nowhere was to be found a scrap of vegetal ornament. There were no acanthus, no tendrils, no leaves, or scrolling plant life gracing the edges of these furnishings—no rosettes. Upon closer examination, even what appeared to be urns were made with straight cylinders, disks, portions of cones, and spheres. In other words, those aspects that appear at first to offer the most literal connection to the formal expression of past ages turn out to have been translated into a contemporary mechanical style. It may not be as blatant as the *ballet méchanique* or Fernand Léger's work of the same period, but it is as intent upon its imagery and method.

This geometric device, handcarved from marble, was used by Pinsent as a finial in lieu of the more traditional globe or urn on several of the low posts outside the villa and on the newel post of the stair in the hall of the villa. It is a twenty-six-sided polygon consisting of eighteen squares and eight triangles that appears in Renaissance prints, paintings, drawings, and marquetry, and obviously relates to geometry, mathematics, optics, and all manner of measurement such as the mapping of globes. When I asked Benedetta Origo if it meant anything in particular to her mother or father, if there was a particular symbolism, she said no, that she didn't think so, that it was "pure Pinsent." I am sure this is true, especially considering that years before he had teased Iris when she was a girl about her ineptness at mathematics in a cartoon he had done of her sailing abilities. Striking in the manner in which they take light and shade, remarkable in their carving by the craftsmen of Rapolano, they stand as an emblem of Pinsent's and the Origos' humanist and intellectual allegiances, as well as the combination of tradition and modernity that infuses all of the architecture and landscape of La Foce.

1 July 98 · La Foce.

many times in Italy. it becomes obvious how important
and dining are as part of the routine, the social dimension
as well as organizing the landscape. Not only are many of the
plants edible or used as spices and seasonings, and nearly
kitchen gardens. but the entire distant landscape is one of
production - wheat fields, orchards, vineyards, groves, etc.

but with one's friends, host, or other guests always comes
mealtime · which can be simple or elaborate but certainly are
seriously and not rushed through. While some may say
Italian food is really very simple. (as some say of Japanese
are —) certainly that doesn't prevent it from being very
artful and refined .. even subtle and often wonderful.

meals thus far : 27 June. Dinner with Morna L. @ the Oasis
(former Dopolavoro). Ravioli w/ sage and truffels, good chicken - good salad
v. best Roasted peppers + melanzanie .
        Sun 28 June . Dinner with Morna @ Castiglioncello
    de Trinoro · Pici (the large eggless spaghetti of the region) with
    Ragu and then Rabbit, salad, macedonia · (w/ olives + fennel !
June. lunch served by Chiara @ La Foce. · A nice pasta (penna) with light
    sauce. followed by a breaded veal · so thin she called it carpacio.
    and Fruit, coffee. Pecorino (3 kinds - old. medium and young)
    Dinner was a zucchinni Fritata after salad etc.

30 June · Benedetta arrives and Dinner by Chiara is a lovely Fusili
    pasta with olives and capers and tomatoes. followed by Guinea Fowl
    from the Estate · Fruit · cheese · coffee
    Salad · beautifully dressed
1 July lunch on terrace w/ friend of Benedetta's - begin with prosciutto
    melone · then a light pasta. penna w/ pomodoro and onions · then
    Salad · a mixed greens (Chinese cabbage lettuce · w/ fennel + celery + onion)
    then cheese and fruit.
    Dinner Benedetta drove us to Rocca D'orcia for a meal in the tiny town
    square · A feast it turns out of various dishes. the first   coppo. penna ·
with sausage was a stuffed goose neck in slices as very subtle salsa verde ! then we decided
or a   to skip pasta. went on to several dishes. Nat had a steak, I had a mixed
veal →   grill of chicken, pork, veal, in a hearty red wine sauce.; Benedetta had a
    v. thin sliced veal (roasted) with a thin sauce. then she had a zucchini
    mousse · very like a cheese souffle ~ and on to salad and desert of Pear Sauce and cheese

— And so it goes. all with good rough bread and the local wines.
  usually white for lunch and red for dinner. the wine at la
  Foce being from the region - most get from near lake Trasimeno
  or from Montalcino. very good indeed.

— · the last lunch @ la Foce was a cold Rice Salad w/ olives, capers,
  tomatoes, herbs chopped fine (superb) followed by cold Salami
  2 kinds · then salad and home made Tuscan prune tart !
  then cheese and coffee.   !

        A curved device of 3 overlapped octagons of squares
        joined by equilateral triangles as to describe a
        globe of sorts. Made of travertine · very handsome as
        they take the light and shade. Large enough to have a
                real presence.

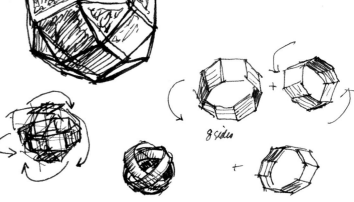

                                        8 sides

This device was used by Pincet · on gate posts out front
of the villa and on the stair newell post in the villa
at the Front Hall. It is an old renaissance device
that appears in prints, paintings, drawings and inlay ·
obviously relating to geometry, mathematics, optics, and
all manner of measurement (mapping of globes etc.)
Pincent seemed fond of (or intrigued by) it · using it here
as an ornament.   When I asked Benedetta if it meant
anything particular to her Father or Mother , some symbolism,
            she said. "no. she didn't think so". she
            said it was " pure pincent "

The Courtyard and service Buildings created sequentially in 1931, 32 and 33. by The origos and Pinsent. With side garden entry to L

unobtrusive side door entry in Hedge

Estate Office

View out

Family Entry
Workers entry.

Family Entry
"Side Door. to upper level.

The Formal Entry

Public

14. FATTORIA COURTYARD GATE
(PRECEDING, PAGE 210)

After making a habitable residence for the Origos, Pinsent was engaged in the design and construction of the working buildings for the estate—the *fattoria*—sequentially in 1931, 1932, and 1933. In doing so he showed a deep understanding of the vernacular buildings of the region, of their typology and detailed expression. Here he created an archetypal courtyard ensemble to house offices, workrooms, storerooms, a kitchen service wing, and an additional bedroom/residential wing connected to the original "Peruzzi" block. His choice of elements is careful and limited. The work is clear, nearly austere: a square *cortile*, two arched entry gates, plain walls, a few windows, a tile roof, and a water basin for laundry and the watering of animals and plants in the arch in the distance. But it is not as simple as it seems. The arches are not mere semicircles, the simple arcs of the early Renaissance, but rather the compound ones that are found in self-conscious mannerist and baroque compositions. Pinsent's application of this spare stone trim is similar to the use of *pietra serena* by Brunelleschi and San Gallo in the north, or of *tufo* and brick by Peruzzi in Rome and Siena. Furthermore, he utilizes the particular window surround seen in the sketch with rigorous consistency throughout this complex, as well as in the numerous *case coloniche*, the standard workers' housing he executed for the Origos. Through this repetition of clear rectangular forms, uniform surfaces and color of stucco, identical external stairs, window shape and trim detail, the entire estate of thousands of hectares was unified and brought under one conceptual idea and image.

Behind the green wall of cypress, some trimmed and some not, lies an entry garden to both the kitchen wing and the main villa.

Above is a sketch of the wall and cypress screen planting that enclose and separate the villa from the service drive. Below, the incremental growth of the estate offices, work and storage buildings can be seen moving off to the left (north and east) from the original building and its entry. Within the large cypress-enclosed room to the right, adjacent to the entry allée, are the *limonaia*, and the "piazzale," which now holds a swimming pool. This has been a place for family and especially children's recreation since the 1930s.

La Foce . 1 July 98   View from the Loggia at the Breakfast room .

16. VIEW INTO THE GARDEN FROM THE LOGGIA

On the left is the grotto made from laurel—a particularly effective garden seat, cool and shady with a view back to the fountain, house, and rose arbor. The fountain is particularly good. A focal point, it provides the quiet sound of a continuous small drip from the upper basin to the lower. Doves and other smaller songbirds come to the basin constantly to drink and sit perched with their reflections on the rim. Occasionally one will also bathe, splashing about in the sun. The open gate with its plump urns beckons one to get up and come forward to see just what is beyond. Despite the perfection of this sun-filled room, the doorway demands movement, which speaks of the power of such axes when well executed.

The subject of time is introduced in gardens at almost every turn for those who are observant. The growth, age, and death of plants is only the most obvious example. One of the pleasures of drawing—unlike amateur photography (serious work such as that of Morna Livingston's reproduced here is another story, being much more like drawing in its concentration, time-consuming patience, personal expression, and editing)—is that in order to make one, a person has to sit still for a time and actually look carefully at what is there. An example of this was my concentration upon the dolphin fountain in the center of this space. It appears to be and probably is an item purchased early in the development of the gardens, found somewhere in the north and brought here. The basin on the other hand feels completely Pinsent, with its rococo shape, crisp exaggerated profile, and curbed edge at the grass. More than sixty years of filling the villa's reservoir from an aquifer deep within limestone rock formations to supply the water that trickles constantly over the edge of this basin has produced a calcareous beard, a proto-stalactite on its lee side where the nearly constant summer breeze nudges it—the passage of time and movement of water made visible.

Although I had hoped this drawing might capture some of this charm and imperative, I was disappointed with the result. Later I returned to try a watercolor that seems more successful in some ways.

La Foce. 2 July
view from The Break[...]

This watercolor is of the view from inside the relatively new, but seemingly long-established breakfast room. One of the most surprising aspects of good design is how obvious and inevitable a thing can seem once done, though it did not exist at all and had not been thought of by anyone before, even its own author.

From here one sees (and feels) the layers of space created by the diverse elements of this first garden space. These layers are emphasized by the billowing linen curtains moving in the morning breeze, the pergola columns, the sunlight and shadows of roses on the canvas of the arbor above, the group of wicker chairs, fountain, and several sets of hedges in boxwood and laurel, all stepping away and back into space, with the sky and deep space of the Val d'Orcia beyond.

The rose arbor in this small upper garden is an example of the continuous inhabitation and adaptation of the garden since its beginning in 1928. As Pinsent left it with the Origos, it was a narrow L-shaped structure two meters in depth, part of which was taken up by plant beds to provide the pockets for the roses that were trained to grow up the narrow stone columns. As Benedetta Origo pointed out to me, it was always too narrow to use effectively as a terrace, despite the attractive view and garden space. Also, only storerooms along the lower floor of this early addition to the villa abutted it. Upper bedrooms, however, did look out over the roses planted by Iris Origo (Mermaid, a particularly nice flat, white one). Also the total symmetry of the box hedges was a bit claustrophobic. People could, and did, sit in the shade of the green grotto cut out of laurel with its diagonal view back to the villa, however.

In 1990 Benedetta transformed this area by creating a breakfast room in what had been a former storeroom, opening it out with French doors *enfilade* with the original dining room and kitchen. She also moved four of the travertine columns forward into the garden and ripped out a pair of the flanking hedges, transforming this area into a truly useful (and special) outdoor loggia for dining and sitting. This required ordering two more matching columns from Rapolano for the reentrant corners, which a few years later cannot be told from the original. These marble posts are thought-provoking in other ways, as may be seen in an earlier sketch (no. 6). Extremely tall and thin rectangular pieces of stone with the simplest, sharp, stripped-down little capitals, they have tiny crisp arris lines with a fine, flat picked surface. They are extremely refined for structural stone elements, actually having the dimensions and proportions more commonly found in wood posts. The portions of the frame above that supports the crosspieces, which in turn support the rose vines, are also extremely light. For several centuries many architects and scholars have pondered the evolution and derivation of the stone structures of ancient Greek temples, with some speculating that they are probably derived from earlier wooden prototypes, that many of the details are carved stone representations of organic materials: carved timber posts, beams, purlins, fastenings, and bindings. Here at La Foce, Pinsent, an architect who had moved in art-historical circles for decades, has produced a modest structure with stone columns so attenuated that they can only be seen (by those who might notice) as just such a metamorphosis of wood into stone, in itself becoming, therefore, also a thoroughly classical notion.

Another recent development has greatly enhanced the utility and charm of this arbor. In 1998 the canvas hanging in swags beneath the roses was added. Reminiscent of the ancient tradition of awnings pulled across atria and market streets, which can still be found in courtyards and cafés in Greece and other parts of the Mediterranean, these awnings have at least three obvious benefits. First, it allows one to use the terrace during periods of light rain or mist, as arbors are notoriously leaky and less sheltering than they seem. Second, it keeps leaves, petals, and the continuous detritus that sift down from living plants (no matter how beautiful) out of one's soup during meals. Third, it provides a lovely pattern of shadows overhead and a diffuse golden light to the terrace below.

18. LEMON TERRACE WITH OLD STABLE AND CLAY HILLS BEYOND (OVERLEAF)

A view of the lemon terrace seen from the top of the stairs by the barrel vault and rose garden. The original sixteenth-century structure, now the main block of the villa, is on the right. Beyond the garden wall, with its insistent pregnant urns, is the long tile roof of the former stables. Beyond it one sees a parallel clay ridge, a remnant of the *crete senesi* that shape the valley and made agriculture so difficult, preventing for so long its intensive development beyond that of the river bottom and lower slopes.

This garden, in its geometry and architecture, is reminiscent of stepped or terraced rectangles of several of the Medici villas near Florence, including that of the one at Fiesole in which Iris Origo spent significant portions of her youth as she described in *Images and Shadows*. Large terra-cotta pots with lemons are set out in the spring on round stone bases that are permanently located in these compartments. In the autumn they are taken into the *limonaia* (a traditional structure similar and antecedent to the familiar orangeries of the north), located in the piazza adjacent to the entry gate, where they spend the winter.

Each of the terraces is enclosed by boxwood hedges and edged with plants, such as lavender at the cut slopes and banks, with perennials and pomegranates along the south-facing wall to the right. The far wall along the road, seen at this time of day in shade, is covered with a variety of vines—mostly ivy, clematis, honeysuckle. Here have been located several basins for the gardeners to use, one of which is now filled with an exquisite miniature water lily.

In the deep distance, atop the clay ridge one can make out the silhouette of a *casa colonica*, which was in fact one of the very first projects Pinsent engaged in for Antonio Origo—the housing of his *contadini*—a humanitarian and practical act on the one hand, and a territorial assertion on the other. Castelluccio sits upon the ridge above and behind the mass of trees above the villa on the right.

The limonaia. La Foce. 2 July 1998

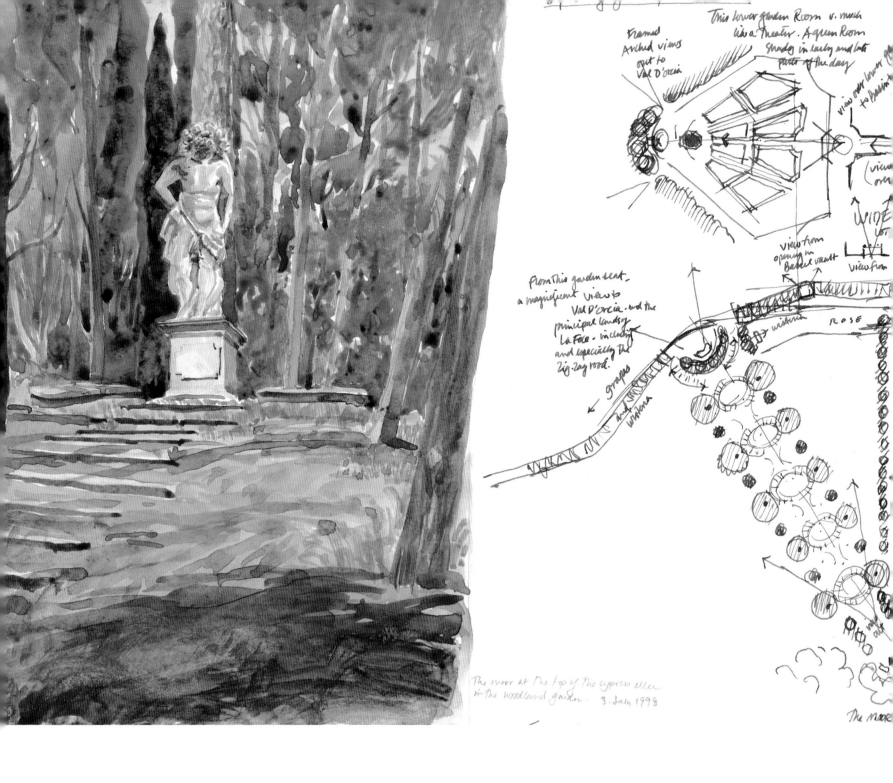

There is also a view back and up
to the Fountain grotto from
the seat at the basin.

This is a broad Horizontal view, however,
unlike the deep, vertical view from the upper
overlook.

Closed. intimate Room
view out from
pergola and
N. wing of Villa

Hills } Here as in some other villa gardens. one almost
steps out into the sky. with the world removed.
A sense of both structure · order. maze like
hedges. combined with that of wide open
spaces.

and Horizon

OPEN

This allee is
mostly a view up.
from below. To
be seen from the lower
garden and villa.

When one walks (climbs) up
the view out is not particularly
back down this allee. But is to
the left. out over a rustic
(rather baroque) allee. now
in a poor state.... ie. the
shrubs and flowers are gone
and the grading has
deteriorated. swallowing up
the steps.

The seat and
statue(s) The octagonal
pool in lower garden.

3 July 1996

The rose garden and the extension of the wisteria arbor called the *voltabotte* (literally, barrel vault) form the uppermost level of the garden terraces. Above this plateau the hillside has been carefully cut into a series of relatively equal terraces, originally for agricultural purposes. The hillside above the Chiarentana road below this arbor and beyond the farthest extent of the lower garden was also terraced in this traditional manner. (See parallel strips on plan between the woods to the north and the garden rooms.) The lower slopes, from the 1930s through the 1950s, were largely devoted to wheat and olives. The upper terraces, originally used as fields for various crops, still contain numerous fruit trees from this period plus recent additions. In a portion above the *fattoria*, an extensive kitchen garden remains.

From this upper level of the garden, two distinct allées climb the hill to converge in a grove of pines and cypresses at an imposing allegorical sculpture of a Moor who is carrying a great basket (a cornucopia of sorts) overflowing with fruits and vegetables. One allée, aligned with a central path that begins in the orthogonal layout of the lemon terraces, climbs straight up the hill between rows of cypresses (see cross section, no. 37). Throughout its entire length, risers of travertine hold sloping earth treads (*perrons*) of what amounts to a giant stair that becomes steeper at its upper end. Beside the base of the Moor are two stone benches. From here one has a limited view back down the hill to the garden between the cypresses. In another direction, that of the other allée, the view opens out to the valley and region.

This second allée is both more rustic and more baroque, comprising a series of curved stairs around elliptical terraces, and planted with alternating pairs of Italian stone pines and cypresses (see cross section, no. 38). Based on shallow depressions that remain on the landings and a handful of relic shrubs nearby, it appears that this allée was once a floral walk with perennials on the elliptical landings and flowering shrubs lining the sides, and wildflowers to the left and right on the hillside terraces beneath the fruit trees. At the base of this hill climb is an apsidal plantation of cypresses that frame another well-located garden seat of Pinsent's which commands a spectacular panorama of the Orcia valley and Monte Amiata beyond, and especially to the opposite ridge with its now oft-photographed zigzag road.

A corresponding allegorical figure is located as the focal point at the far end of the lowest garden, a sloping, sunken enclosed terrace with grotto located as an extension of the axis from the house through the lemon terraces. Here the figure, also a strapping young male, is a Caucasian staggering under the burden of construction implements. In this case Pinsent placed the figure upon a base that is also an elaborate seat from which one can obtain a view back up the sloped garden, an intensely green room of boxwood hedges and walls of cypress, to the fountain grotto, stair, and overlook. Whereas the verticality of the upper figure is emphasized by the long foreground stairs and allées of trees, here, through the device of reflection in a small octagonal basin stretched in the direction of the view (either way), Pinsent brilliantly emphasizes verticality in the direction of the statue and horizontality in the direction of the grotto.

20. THE CYPRESS ALLÉE (OVERLEAF)

It is a commonplace to note that landscapes are dynamic, not static, and that it takes years for landscape designs to mature. Today, more than sixty years after much of this garden was planned, laid out, and first planted, some portions are beautifully mature, while others are beginning to need more than mere maintenance, but also renewal, repair, or replacement. A case in point is the replanting in 1999 of significant portions of the cypress allée leading to the statue of the Moor on the hill. Although largely fortuitous, an instructive aspect of this project was the retention of a handful of the old—not yet too far gone—cypresses in a diagonally alternating pattern at intervals (as shown in the plan elevation and perspective) so as to allow one to read the full spatial form of the allée when mature, even though the bulk of it now consists of small, young trees that will not reach maturity for several decades.

16 June 1999. Replanting cypress in the allee, was two chins. La Foce

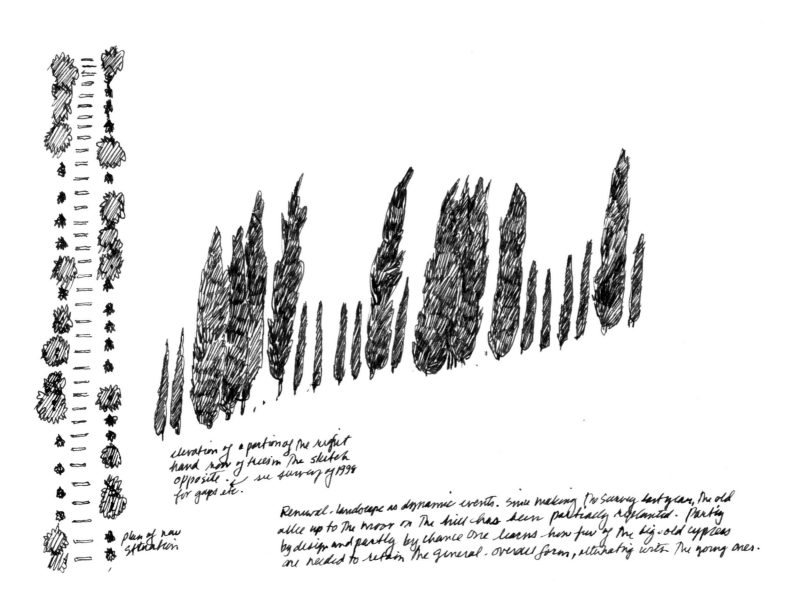

elevation of a portion of the right
hand row of trees in the sketch
opposite — see survey of 1998
for gaps etc.

plan of new
plantation

Renewal. Landscape as dynamic events. Since making the survey last year, the old
allée up to the moor on the hill has been partially replanted. Partly
by design and partly by chance one learns how few of the big old cypress
are needed to retain the general. overall form, alternating with the young ones.

← The English
garden designer now
helping Benedetta who
lives nearby @ Cetona.

In contrast to the vertical deep view of this lower garden as seen fro
top. when seated beyond the octagon pool. looking back, it is a long low
- wide. horizontal scene - with ground plane tilted up - lots of sky. e

Notice how the cypresses have been added to the left to give balance and
the echo of symmetry to the towering wall and line on the right -
A very skillful piece. Also note that the grotto with the fountain is on
only places in the garden without a seat or bench. Why? Because it is fo
sound and affect: not to inhabit necessarily. it isn't really a pri
place to sit. vis-a-vis views etc. v. interesting.

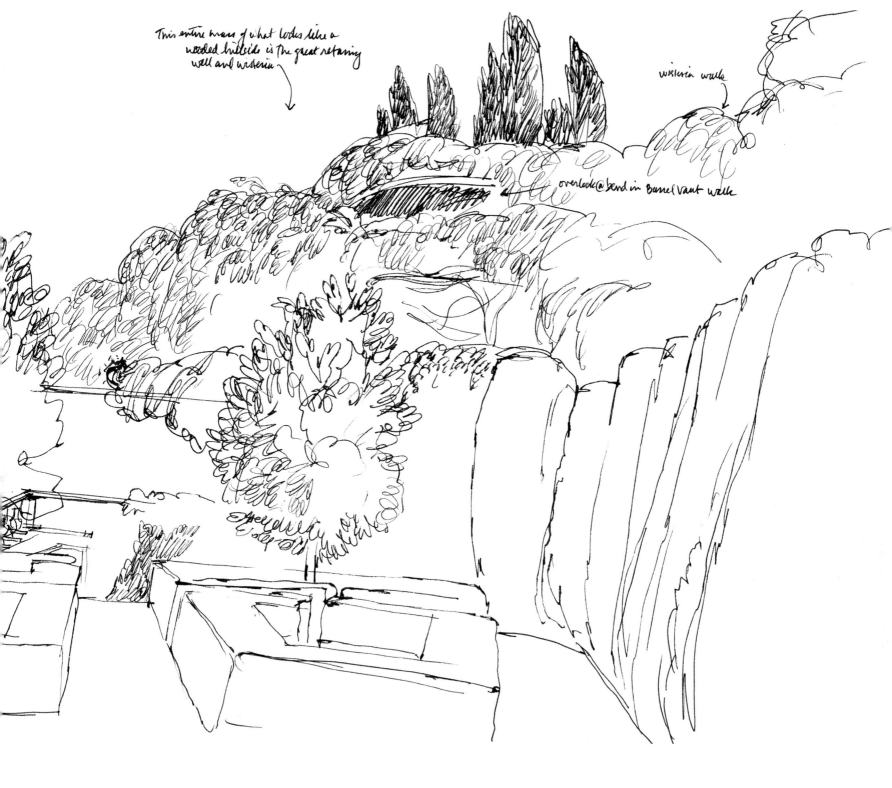

This entire mass of what looks like a
wooded hillside is the great retaining
wall and wisteria

wisteria walk

overlook @ bend in Bunel vaut walk

229

21. LOWER GARDEN WITH GROTTO
(PRECEDING)

In contrast to the deep vertical view of this lower garden from the top of the overlook, this sketch conveys in part the nature of the view beyond the octagonal pool that is obtained from the seat beneath the allegorical figure. It is a wide horizontal scene, with the ground plane tilted up, an imposing grotto with fountain and stairs. Paths lead away in several directions, and the sky becomes an active participant in the composition. The villa and the rest of the world have disappeared. A group of cypresses has been added on the left to give balance and a sense of symmetry to the towering wall and hill on the right. It is a very skillful piece of work. Also note that the fountain grotto is one of the only places in the garden without a seat or bench. Why, one wonders? Most likely it was to contribute sound and scenographic effect, not necessarily to be inhabited. Given views to it and from on top of it, rather than from within, it is not a very privileged place to sit.

The ground is green (grass), the hedges are green (boxwood), the walls are green (cypresses) except for the travertine backdrop and grotto, the trees are green (magnolia grandiflora and cypresses). Except for when the enormous mass of wisteria on the hillside retaining wall and curving arbor above is in bloom, this is about as monochromatic and architectonic as one can get, and quintessentially represents the idea of traditional Italian Renaissance gardens that was held until recent scholarship established how much richer they were in terms of flowering plants. Although Iris Origo was very much in touch with the developments in English gardening of the period by people such as Vita Sackville-West and Gertrude Jekyll (as her own planting of most of the upper garden and terrace shows), this particular place, like the lower garden of the Berensons at I Tatti, also by Pinsent, shows his desire to create something in the grand manner of sixteenth- and seventeenth-century gardens as they were known, measured, and published by architects and landscape architects in the 1920s and 1930s. While not as odd or cartoonlike as the re-creations of American colonial gardens that were made at Williamsburg at this same time, it is an interesting example of one era looking at another. As in all cases where someone is working within a tradition, but is of necessity or desire having to invent not copy, what is different is as interesting as what is alike.

22. PINSENT'S GROTTO DETAILS AND OVERALL GARDEN LAYOUT DIAGRAM (OVERLEAF)

Pinsent was surely a very personal, quirky, even peculiar architect when making structures. One description might be that he was mannerist or baroque at the least. Look at the details in his magnum opus here at the fountain grotto: large, flat architectural details and profiles; reductive shapes boldly drawn on the planes *alla* Carlo Maderna. And then look at these large, chunky rusticated blocks used for the keystone and arches or in the center of the panels *alla* Giulio Romano. There is a mixing of scales and distortion of familiar parts. The proportions of the newel posts on this rather grand double stair with its unusual rusticated obelisks are most peculiar. It is masculine, willful, and idiosyncratic in the extreme.

While working on this drawing, I was struggling with my favorite fountain pen, which had partly broken on the first day of my visit. The pen finally snapped in half, with two more days of work to go on this drawing. Various ballpoint pens and felt-tipped pens available were below par, and a trip to a major city in search of a replacement would have taken too much time.

23. THE FOUNTAIN (FOLLOWING OVERLEAF)

More restoration, seen in the recent repair of Pinsent's tall and lyrical fountain in the grotto of the lower garden. The sound of the small amount of recirculated water fills this cool, tall room, which must be the cleanest, whitest, lightest grotto ever. Here we see Pinsent at his most refined, consistent in his detailing, and extremely successful in updating traditional motifs. Note how he develops what at first seems the common shape of the petals of each of the various basins. On close inspection one finds his love of geometry and the slight deco manner of expressing line and form. Each basin has been developed from an octagonal plan with alternating straight and curved edges and surfaces.

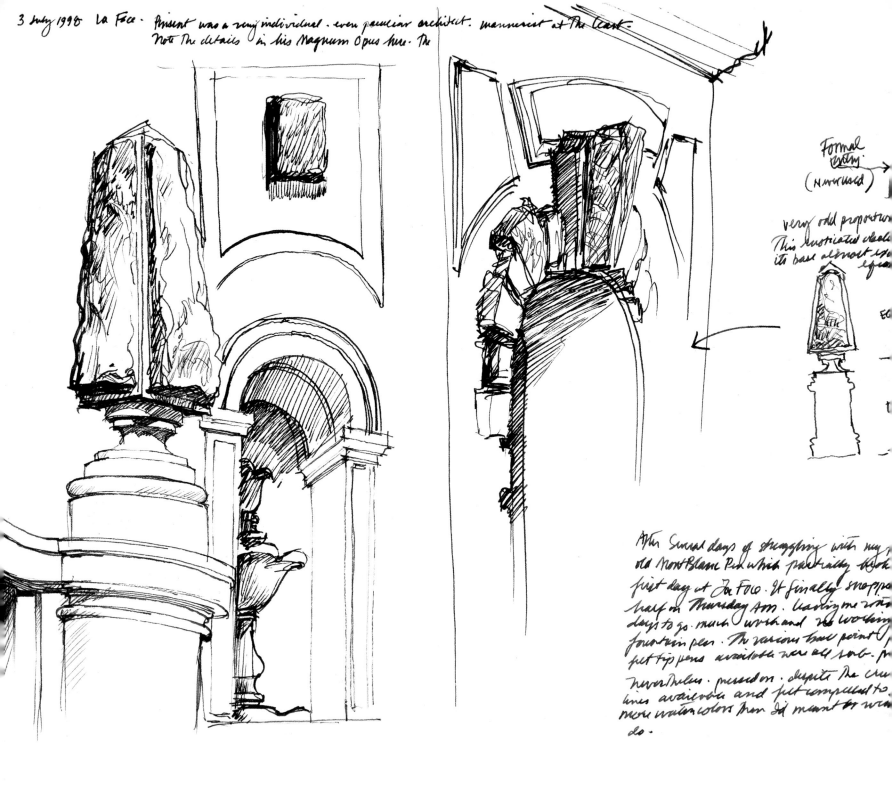

3 July 1998   La Foce. Present was a very individual - even peculiar architect. mannerist at the least. Note the details in his Magnum Opus here. The

Formal entry. (Never used)

very odd proportion
This rusticated clad...
its base almost exc...
equa...

After several days of struggling with my
old Mont Blanc Pen which partially brok...
first day at La Foce. It finally snappe...
half on Thursday AM. leaving me two
days to go. much work and the working
fountain pen. The various true point fe...
felt tip pens available were all soft. ...
Nevertheless. pressed on. despite the cru...
lines available and felt compelled to ...
more watercolors than I'd meant to ...
do.

232

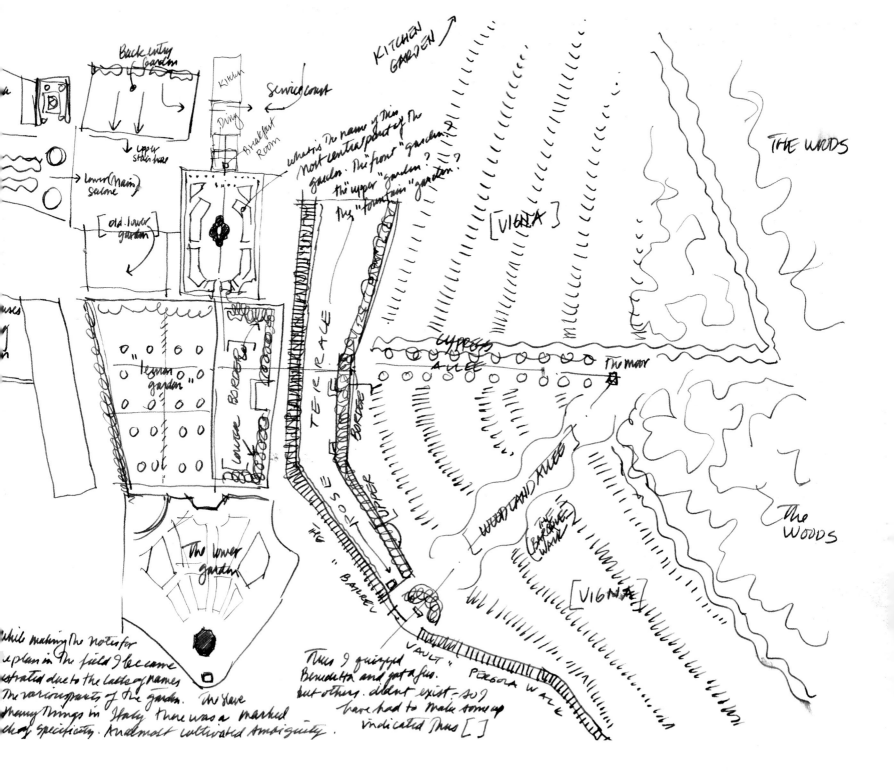

Back entry garden

Kitchen

Dining

Breakfast Room

Service court

Upper staircase

Lower (main) saline

old lower garden

what is the name of this most central part of the garden. The "front" garden? the "upper" garden? the "fountain" garden?

KITCHEN GARDEN

THE WOODS

[VIGNA]

"lemon garden"

lemon border

CYPRESS ALLEE

The moor

TERRACE

WOODLAND ALLEE

THE WOODS

The lower garden

The "BARREL"

VAULT

THE BAROQUE WALK

[VIGNA]

PERGOLA WALK

While making the notes for the plan in the field I became frustrated due to the lack of names the various parts of the garden. The have many things in Italy there was a marked their specificity. And almost cultivated ambiguity.

Thus I quizzed Benedetta and got a few but others didn't exist — so I have had to make some up indicated thus [ ]

233

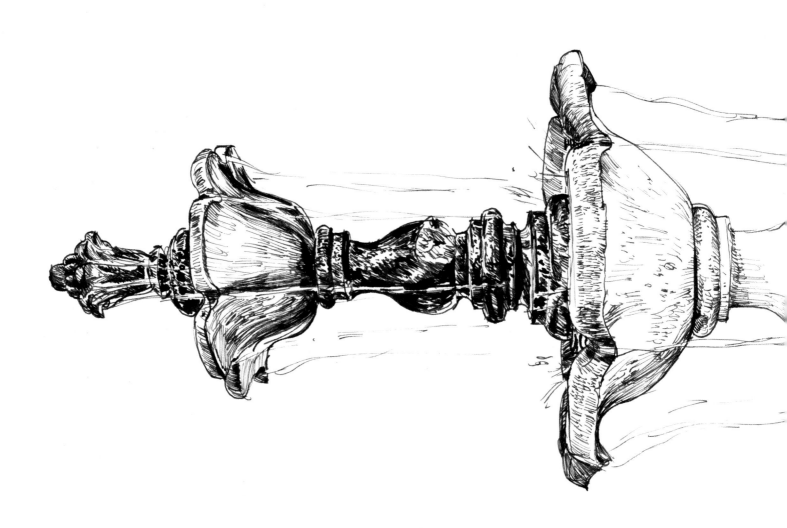

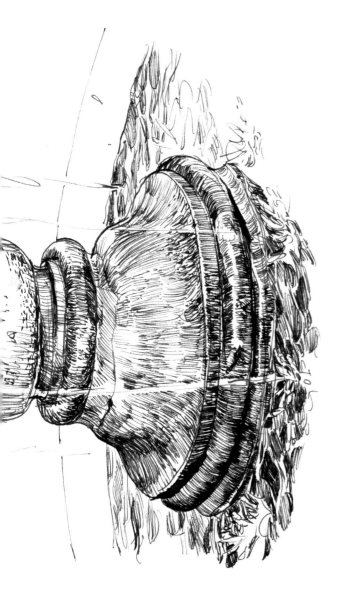

16 Aug 1995 –

The fountain in the lower garden. Never functioned – le Feu.
Here in Paris white again – The radiant, lightest gesture ever. We
see Prince at his most refined – Christian in his detailing yet
strangely successful in updating the old standard. I especially
like the not overly common shape of the petals of the various
basins

Here we see presents form of geometry –

It an octagon pattern really in the form
of a traditional fountain.

235

4 July 1998

Although I thought this long pergola (210 m) was extremely handsome and the rose garden pleasant upon first seeing them, I didn't pay them as much attention as other parts of the garden. There are some bed shapes that don't seem as effective as others; some colors not quite as certain as others. However, they grow upon you, gradually revealing themselves to be very special. First there is the unprecedented arbor that goes on and on, that wanders along, turns corners, goes down hill, around a bend, down some more, finally ending at the woods where path goes off, and on one learns to the family cemetery. Thus an act of arrigo's putting down roots and tying house to garden to land to history. The arbor is beguilingly simple. It hardly seems substantial enough. But then by now the wisteria vines are bigger and stronger, and the folded back quality surprises and pleases, it leads one on. To know this garden one has

The rose garden also, in its own and the folded back quality surprises and pleases, it leads one on. To know this garden one has. To keep exploring it. The layers, lavender and hollyhocks, between the columns, backup the deep, blood red roses. Then in the middle of this rose, eventually leading to coral and white. While all along the upper wall - a vast, taller, border of a great assortment. Benedetta remarked - This is a most "English" part of the garden and in many ways a reflection of her mother's background - (the Medici villa @ Fiesole) but the Anglo-Irish part, and the legacy of the Edwardian gardens of the previous generation, and of Vita S.W. and Jensen's efforts in the era before the war. While I am not v. proud of this weakish sketch, it does record a key part of the garden in par

236

Although I thought that this long arbor (210 meters in length!) was extremely handsome and that the rose garden was pleasant upon first seeing them, I did not pay as much attention to them as to other parts of the garden for a while. There are some bed shapes that do not seem as effective as others, some colors not quite as certain as others. However, this ensemble and its parts grow on you, gradually revealing themselves to be very special. First there is the unprecedented arbor that goes on and on, that wanders along, turns corners, goes downhill, around a bend, down some more, and finally ends at the woods where a path goes off and onward—as one learns—to the family cemetery. In this one structure we see the simple and profound act of the Origos putting down roots, tying house to garden, garden to land, land to history. The arbor is beguilingly simple (see plan, and the longitudinal section [no. 39] where a portion of it shows in elevation). There is nothing quite like it anywhere. It needs to be experienced to be believed or understood. No drawing, painting, or photograph can convey its movement and remarkable extension. Yet it does not seem grandiose. It hardly seems substantial enough with its simple wooden posts and thin metal hoops—but then by now the wisteria vines, in some cases approaching seventy years in age, are so substantial that they seem to be holding the pergola up. As Morna Livingston's photographs indicate, it is an absolute vision and overpowering olfactory event in the spring. When I asked Benedetta Origo what this feature was called, she said to me in Italian, "the barrel vault."

The rose garden, also, in its length and run, and in its folded quality that both hides its extent (that is, either end from the other), surprises and pleases. Like the great arbor, in smaller scope with more difficult plants it leads one on, and in season can overpower with color and fragrance. To know this garden one has to move, to keep exploring its layers. There is a delicious combination of lavender and hollyhocks between the arbor posts that form a backdrop for a continuous bed of deep blood-red roses. Then in the beds down the middle are more of this rose, eventually leading to coral and white. Meanwhile, all along the wall against the hill extends a vast, taller border of a great assortment of herbaceous plants, perennials, and shrubs. As Benedetta remarked, this is a most "English" part of the garden, and in many ways is a reflection of her mother's background—not the Medici villa at Fiesole part, but the Anglo-Irish part, and the legacy of Edwardian gardens of the previous generation such as Sissinghurst, Hidcote, and Hestercombe. Although I am not very proud of this weakish sketch, it does record some aspects of this key portion of the garden.

22 July 1999. The upper garden. Rose Terrace. La Foce. Roses like it hot and I am a test that this terrace is hot. As I drew this I roasted.

This central portion of the Rose Terrace with Pinsent's stairs against the wall anchors the other parts. which fold back from it.

Geraniums and lavender above. Roses, lavender, hollyhocks and wisteria below.

To the right is the terraced *vigna* with its fruit trees and woodland. To the left is the barrel-vault pergola with its wisteria vines underplanted with a superb combination of lavender and roses (with hollyhocks and other things mixed in). When I first studied this area I did not understand several aspects, namely, the shape and layout of the beds, the seeming lack of resolution of the northern end adjacent to the villa, and the twin stairways. Later I discovered that Pinsent had originally planted a group of cypresses to terminate this end, thereby matching the opposite southern end, framing it dramatically and symmetrically (see no. 26). Furthermore, he had also placed a large stone bench as a twin to the similar (but different) one now seen at the other end of the rose terrace (see no. 12). This has since been moved to the piazza, where it now faces the *limonaia* (see no. 28). This pair of groves and seats was then echoed by these two handsome stone steps which further frame the center of this elongated and bent terrace, creating a transverse axis with their invitation to leave the most cultivated (and English) portions of the garden to stroll up the hill into the looser, more Italian agrarian part, in turn suggesting the gradient of artifice and situation of the "garden within the park."

Aerial view of the rose terrace with a reconstruction of the missing cypress grove at the north end of this space, indicating the centrality of the portion with the two small stone stairs and the cross-axes of the cypress allée and this framing device.

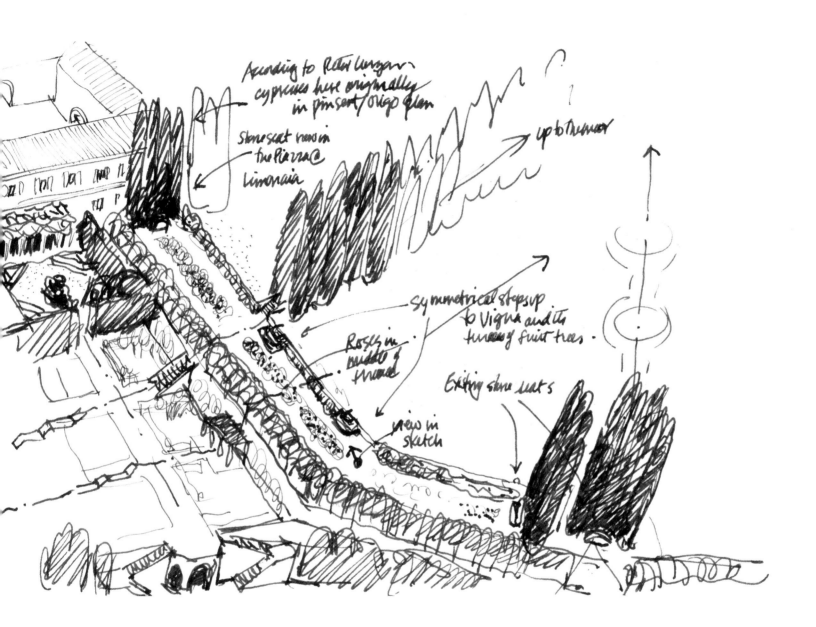

According to Peter Ungar,
cypresses here originally
in pinsent/Origo plan

Stone seat new in
the Piazza @
Limonaia

up to the manor

symmetrical steps up
to Vigna and its
terrace of fruit trees.

Roses in
middle of
thread

Existing stone seats

view in
sketch

27. AN OLD WELL (OR CISTERN) HEAD FROM CASTELLUCCIO IN THE CORTILE OF THE FATTORIA

28. THE LIMONAIA IN MODERN LIFE (OVERLEAF)

Although many large pots of citrus and other tender plants are still kept within this traditional south-facing building through the cold and often snowy winters, in summer it serves as the swimming pavilion for several generations of the descendants of Iris and Antonio Origo when they gather at La Foce. Notable is the combination of traditional service building with its nearly industrial doors and glazing with Pinsent's theatrical sense of overscale ornament and the luxuriant mass of jasmine vines that heavily perfume the air of this summery space.

well head from Castellaccio brought down to La Foce by Antonio Origo · to place in the courtyard of the Fattoria of Plisent's design.
drawing this workmen were painting the platforms and erecting lights for the Sunday opening concert of "Incontri di Foce..for this year.

La Foce. The Limonaia in
modern life. The Piazza now
a busy swimming pool. 19 July 1999
Daughters. Granddaughters. Husbands.
Children, cousins and friends around.
In the pool. Soccer balls on the lawn.
Babies, telephones, books, and afternoon
tea as the shadows lengthen.

An astonishing growth of
jasmine on the panels between
and over the great arched
doors and windows that
gives a heavy and sweet
smell to the afternoon air

244

La Foce - 20 July 1999. The old Stables and historic road to Chiarancciona and Scienna from The via Cascici in The Orcia valley below. Nowadays only to go to Chiarentana and Castiglioncello del Trinoro and Cetona. With The high garden wall of The lemon terraces to The right.

Here next to The road on The little tower at The entry one finds The coat of arms of The Mieli family The former owners. It's a bee hive and 3 bees, as The Italian word for Honey is Mieli.

The old stables and historic road to Chianciano, Montepulciano, Pienza, and eventually Siena from the Via Cassia in the Orcia valley below, now used only to go to Chiarentana, Castiglioncello del Trinoro, and Cetona. The high wall on the right supports the rectangular lemon terraces of La Foce. The pen-and-ink sketch is of a travertine plaque found on the little tower adjacent to the villa entry gate representing the coat of arms of the Mieli family, former owners of the villa. It depicts a beehive and three bees (the Italian word for honey is *miele*).

One of the cluster of social service structures designed by Pinsent as part of the estate. The crossroad and entry gate with its piers and cypress allées can be seen just up the hill beyond. Downhill and to the right just out of this sketch are located the school and Casa dei Bambini. Today all three buildings are used as residences because they have been replaced by larger modern facilities nearby in Chianciano.

22 July '99. The Ambulatorio Gianni Origo. and the road leading up to the crossroad and the entry to La Foce. The Villa gates. To the right below the

"Hind the Pines are the Casa Bambini and the School →"

Big white Dog at the Ambulatorio objecting to my presence. Now a residence for Estate staff families.

When I showed this drawing to the Estate manager who's office is in the Fattoria @ La Foce. He told me he'd been kept as a baby in the Casa dei Bambini. Born at Castiglioncello del Trinoro and had risen through effort, schooling at La Foce and Chianciano to being the head of the business for the Estate. He's name = Alfiero Mazzuoli. Traffic here is now terrific - and the number of people who stop at the crossroads to puzzle out which way to go seems high. Trucks, cars, workers, rush back and forth, turning, honking and passing on.

The roadside verges here are full of the usual weeds - convolvulus (bind weed), nettles, chicory, mulberry, a brush form of oak, dock, etc...

This is the view from the upper garden, several terraces, and the overlooks at La Foce. It is the zigzag road with cypresses that now appears on postcards in every shop and every photo book on Tuscany. It has become a symbol of the region, yet it was only recently invented and built by Antonio Origo to give access to the land that he and his workers were reclaiming from the waste, the barren clay hillsides. One can see three of the new *case coloniche*, the farmhouses designed and built by Pinsent—two along the road as it ascends, and one off to the right on the ridge. When I mentioned how picturesque it was, and what an important and integral part of the visual composition, Benedetta Origo rather firmly told me that no one builds a road for mere visual effect, that it is too much of an effort and commitment. At another time she mentioned how limited her parents' resources were in the first early years of their efforts before her mother's windfall inheritance that allowed them to embark on many of the later projects at both the villa and garden and the larger estate. The Ospedale and the Casa dei Bambini received aid from various programs of the fascist government, even though they were heartfelt and deeply personal reform improvements initiated by the Origos. So, too, certain of Antonio Origo's agricultural, water, and land reclamation projects received financial assistance. But many of the most fundamental improvements, such as this road, were simply early and lasting symbols of Origo's commitment to the land, the people, and his family. There is no question that there is a moral dimension to this work, but likewise there is a deep aesthetic one. The two are inextricable. In this scene and in the life of Iris and Antonio Origo, the sense that Tuscany is beautiful because it is cultivated, worked, constructed, and that such work and construction, the reclaiming of wastes and agricultural effort, are artistic and civic activities cannot be escaped. It is no accident that a road they needed was placed thus, opposite La Foce, to be seen daily as a reminder of this truth, and that likewise from it one can see La Foce.

20 July 99. Ploughing under the stubble of the first crop for the second one of the summer. The farms of La Foce, looking toward Radicofani across the Orcia valley. The noise and smell are powerful. From a distance the roar of the engines, closer the clanking of the metal cleats of the tractor tracks, and then the powerful smell of the fresh turned earth. The heavy clay loam of the Val D'Orcia. They still plough strips in concentric manner as they did with ox...

254

32. THE ESTATE

Antonio Origo's investment in the agricultural future of the lands surrounding La Foce continues to bear fruit today. As in much of the Orcia valley, these farmers are engaged in plowing under the stubble of the first harvest of wheat in mid-July in preparation for the second planting of the summer using equipment and methods pioneered on these heavy clay soils by Origo sixty years ago.

33. CHIARENTANA (OVERLEAF)

This ancient fortified farm was once an integral portion of La Foce's agricultural estate housing numerous families of *contadini*.

18 July 1999   Chiarentana . La Foce . Hot, very hot this afternoon . Drone of cicadas all afternoon . Birds constantly calling

ods in the ravine below. Swallows flittering back and forth over the lawn and fields, scooping up insects in the heat.

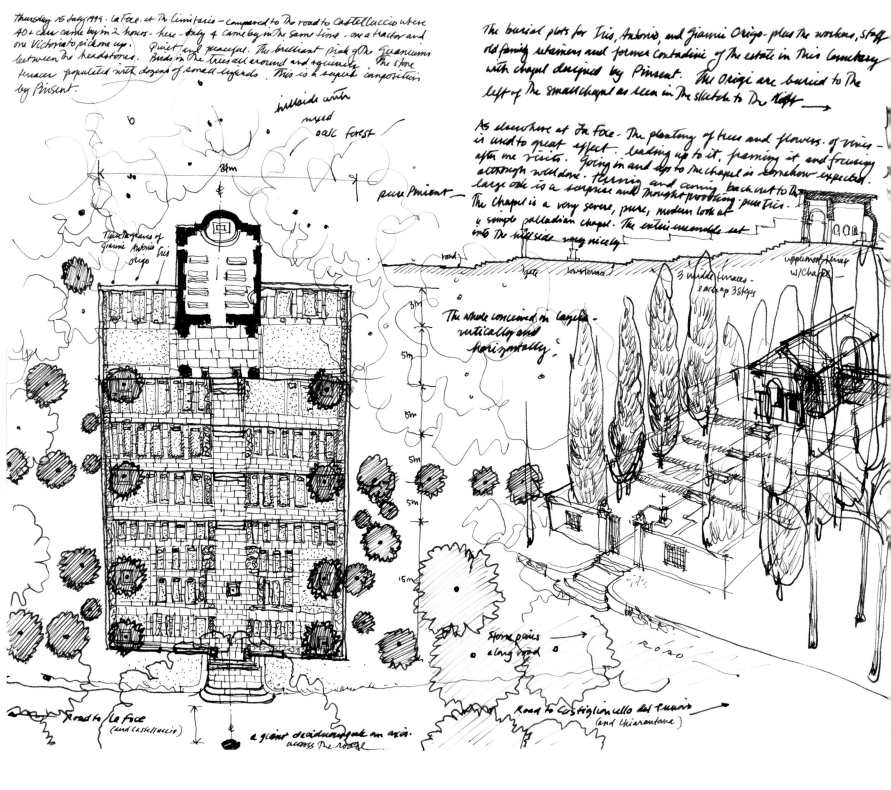

Thursday 15 July 1999. La Foce. at The Cimitario – Compared to The road to Castelluccio where 40+ cars came by in 2 hours – here – only 4 came by in the same time. on a tractor and one Victoriato pick me up. Quiet and peaceful. The brilliant pink of The Geraniums between The headstones. Birds in The trees all around and squirrels. The stone terraces populated with dozens of small lizards. This is a superb composition by Pinsent.

The burial plots for Iris, Antonio, and Gianni Origo. plus The workers, staff, old family retainers and former contadini of The estate in This Cemetery with chapel designed by Pinsent. The Origi are buried to The left of The small chapel as seen in The sketch to The Right →

As elsewhere at La Foce. The planting of trees and flowers. of vines – is used to great effect. leading up to it, framing it and focusing after me visits. Going in and up to The chapel is somehow expected although well done. Turning and coming back out to The large oak is a surprise and thought provoking. pure Iris. The Chapel is a very severe, pure, modern look at a simple palladian chapel. The entire ensemble set into The hillside very nicely.

hillside with mixed oak forest

pure Pinsent

Three the graves of Gianni Antonio Iris Origo

Road to La Foce (and Castelluccio)

a giant deciduous oak on axis. across The road

The whole conceived in layers – vertically and horizontally.

road

gate

sottostrada

3 middle terraces – each up 38 steps

uppermost terrace w/ Chapel

stone piers → along road

Road to Castiglioncello del Trinoro (and Chiarentana) →

rose

15 July 1999. The cemetery at La Foce

Plan and diagrams depicting Pinsent's brilliantly worked out and beautifully sited composition for the cemetery at La Foce that exploits a sequential terracing and layers of trees, walls, and terraces to set up the small, austere, and forceful chapel. The burial plots of Iris, Antonio, and Gianni Origo are to the left of the chapel on the uppermost terrace. Over time numerous workers, staff, old family retainers, and former *contadini* of the estate have also been buried here.

As elsewhere at La Foce, the planting of trees and flowers as well as vines is used to great effect leading up to and framing the cemetery in general and the chapel in particular. This anticipation and focus as one enters and approaches the chapel are to be expected. A surprise, however, is the unanticipated discovery, upon turning to leave and descend toward the gate, that the entire composition has been centered on the location of an old and singular oak tree immediately opposite the entry. The composition that so clearly framed the chapel now does so for this powerful presence.

The chapel is a severe, pure, and modern essay on a simple Palladian motif. The entire ensemble is tightly knit, positioned and adjusted to the multiple curves of the hill exquisitely.

2 · 20 July 1999 · Cimitero. The Great Oak, opposite the Entrance.

261

35. THE OAK TREE (PRECEDING)

What could speak more to the continuity of life—the ancient concept of resurrection and the eternal cycles of life, birth, growth, death, and rebirth—than this majestic oak tree that greets one upon looking back out from the chapel or on leaving the cemetery. A deciduous tree, it stands bare (and dead looking) against the sky and bitterly cold, distant hills all winter, only to burst into leaf again each spring. It speaks eloquently of life and plenty even in the presence of loss and death. It is a brilliant stroke and shows how insightful and poetic the Origos and their architect were in the location and design of this superb family graveyard.

While drawing I had the pleasurable company and constant chattering and calls of songbirds in the trees and adjacent woodland and a wealth of small lizards who love the warm stones of the cemetery. Bees and butterflies plied the flowers, while just below and across the road tractors clattered back and forth plowing the wheat fields (see no. 32).

36. CROSS SECTION ALONG ENTRY ALLÉE AND VILLA (OVERLEAF)

In this drawing one sees the length of the entry allée with the gate and little tower built here, and one of the trimmed ilex (live oak) pair that frame the entry and piazza. This portion of the villa, with entry loggia and its superb two-story central *salone* and sometime dining room with frescoes and skylight, was designed by Pinsent within the shell of the sixteenth-century structure. Although there was (and is) a garden room directly beyond the ground-floor *salone*, it is small and cramped. The first important garden room completed here was that on the left, a composition of hedges with the dolphin fountain and green grotto. The rose arbor in its original narrow form still exists against this portion of the villa. Above this garden can be seen the rose garden with the wisteria arbor on its right and the beginning of the *vigna* with its cut terraces on the far left.

The wing of the building facing the small garden with the dolphin fountain immediately behind the lemon terraces is the first addition that Pinsent and the Origos added to the sixteenth-century structure on the far left. The wisteria arbor, or "barrel vault," and rose terrace are immediately above the lemon terraces. The Moor can be seen at the extreme right at the top of the stair and cypress allée.

An area of live oaks above the lower grotto garden is seen at the extreme left below the garden seat and cypress apse that overlooks the valley at a break in the wisteria arbor. The rustic, somewhat baroque stair and allée that ascend the hill through what was in effect the *vigna* lead to the allegorical figure of the Moor in a grove of pines and cypress at the upper left.

39. LONGITUDINAL SECTION FROM VILLA TO THE LOWER GARDEN, GROTTO, AND BASIN (FOLLOWING OVERLEAF)

On the left is the garden room with the dolphin fountain, hedges, and the green grotto. Next come the lemon terrace with boxwood cut in bands and hemispheres that lead to the overlook atop the fountain grotto in the lower garden (on the right). Here one sees the sloping plateau that leads to the octagonal basin and bench with its allegorical figure of architecture and backdrop of cypress and live oak, all of which are held up on a major retaining wall. Immediately above these garden rooms can be seen the long horizontal band of the "barrel vault," the lengthy wisteria arbor that eventually winds down and away to the right and out of sight. Above this can be seen the two allées rising through the hillside terraces, recently reclaimed and brought back within the realm of cultivation and management. The cypress stair can be seen rising straight up from the lemon terraces, while the "baroque" allée moves diagonally from the right up to the left to meet at the top of the other. In the background can be seen the woods rising on the hill behind toward the site of the water reservoir. Cypresses that line a local road that skirts around the villa grounds can be seen on the upper left.

Cecil Pinsent and the Making of La Foce

"A PATTERN OF THE WORLD AS HE WOULD HAVE IT"

"LA FOCE WAS AT ITS BEST, garden & landscape," wrote Cecil Pinsent, its designer, on 31 May 1948. Pinsent had called at La Foce on his roundabout and leisurely way to Percy Lubbock's house at Lerici after staying with Bernard Berenson at I Tatti (figure 1) outside Florence.[1] His letter is a straightforward "bread and butter" letter (as they were called), thanking Berenson for his hospitality, passing on news of one Anglo-Saxon resident to another, and in the process touching on one of the topics dear to them all, gardens. Perhaps there was also some *sotto voce* pride, as Pinsent reports to the owner of one garden he had created the continuing delights and success of another, perhaps the most accomplished of his designs.

"La Foce was at its best, garden & landscape." This remark, obvious as it is simple, must have occurred to many visitors to La Foce. For it is impossible to think of the immediate garden there without the larger landscape,[2] or, conversely, to know this sector of the Tuscan landscape in the Val d'Orcia without seeing the garden as its inspired and logical epitome. This is one of many meditations that La Foce must trigger in its visitors' minds, along with other thematic pairs: the garden's enduring modernity as well as its debts to historical traditions of Tuscan garden art; its studied and careful design, along with an apparent nonchalance and lack of posturing; its bookishness, so to speak, and its links to Anglo-Saxon writing on landscape architecture that came out of Tuscany before World War I, yet its constant originality; its wholly contrived spaces, yet its abundant relish of the natural: "it is artificial yet operates at the same time naturally."[3] Also apparent are its quick appeal to visitors here and now, but also its astonishing resilience over innumerable visits as well as in the generous spaces of memory; its relish of form, of materials, as well as its appeal to poetic instincts.

To understand fully the scope and success of La Foce, we need to consider briefly both Pinsent's own career and in particular his other principal garden designs for I Tatti and Le Balze.[4] Born in Uruguay in 1884 of British parents, he was educated at Marlborough, the Architectural Association and the Royal Academy School of Architecture in London, and by extensive European travel.[5] He was introduced to Bernard and Mary Berenson in 1907, thus beginning a career as architect and designer to a group of Anglo-American expatriates in Tuscany, although he went back and forth to England for a couple of years. In 1909 Pinsent started working for the Berensons in partnership with Geoffrey Scott, a recent Oxford graduate who had enrolled in the Architectural Association for only one term; he would essentially function as Pinsent's aesthetic adviser.[6] By the spring of 1912 Pinsent had designed the villa and gardens at Le Balze on the southern slope of Fiesole for Charles Augustus Strong, a Harvard friend of Berenson's.

Le Balze, which survives in the possession of Georgetown University, occupies a narrow platform of land along the hillside. Two gardens (*giardini segreti*) were installed on either side of the house; through the first, one enters the property; from the second, visitors encounter a more open terrace and a fine view toward Florence.[7] The ground drops sharply away from the terrace that runs along the south side of the house; both those slopes and the very narrow space between the north façade and the abrupt hillside are negotiated,

FIGURE 2. Villa Le Balze, first, entry garden. Photograph by the author.

respectively, by terraced vineyards and an elaborate, divided staircase with niches, busts, and extensive pebblework. The situation of the property is impressive, and Pinsent clearly designed the narrow gardens with their exaggerated sense of inwardness to contrast with that openness of vistas (figure 2).[8] Especially the spaces of the first, entry garden, on which a second-floor open portico looks down, are neat and tightly controlled by the geometry of hedge, flower bed, and clipped shrub: it presents an immediate air of Tuscanness—reminiscences, say, of garden spaces depicted in Gustave Utens' lunettes of Medici villas of 1599[9]—yet at the same time is altogether smart and tidy, in an appropriate and modern American way. However, the pebble-encrusted stairs,

niches, and busts at the back of the house (figure 3) are much more playful, both in their self-conscious imitation, despite the restricted space, of a famil-iar Italianate garden feature, and in their exuberant decoration, which some-how draws attention to the slightly implausible effect, at once modern and mannerist, of the whole.

Pinsent's other major garden design was for the Berensons at Settignano, though during 1911 Pinsent and Scott also worked at the Villa Medici, Fiesole, for Lady Sybil Cutting, Iris Origo's mother. This was another impressive, not to say historical, site, and with more ample terraces than at Le Balze (the lower Medici one at least probably survives in Pinsent's version, figure 4). The grounds of I Tatti posed yet other challenges to Pinsent. On the negative side, Berenson's views were not as striking as Strong's or Lady Sybil's (or as would be found at La Foce); more crucially, the main axis of the garden passed through a *limonaia* that stretched across its whole width immediately below the first terrace; the situation and extent of this lemon house effectively de-termine, on the one hand, the width of the gardens designed below it[10] and, on the other, the interruption of the descending site (figure 5). However, the

FIGURE 4. The lower terrace at the Villa Medici, Fiesole. Photograph by the author.

FIGURE 5. Villa I Tatti, main garden below the *limonaia*. Photograph by the author.

territory of I Tatti was extensive enough to incorporate landscapes other than the garden into the overall design in ways that were denied Pinsent at Le Balze. The contrast of shaped and strict intervention within the garden proper could be contrasted with the groves or *boschetti* that surround it and with views onto agricultural land that these woodland walks allow in their turn. The walks, too, could be given different forms: the allée that descends along the left-hand side of the gardens is straight and controlled (see figure 1); the access and paths through meadows to the right are more relaxed and tend to follow the contour lines.

In all, I Tatti is a more imposing design than Le Balze, with a grave and almost imperious central series of compartmented terraces. Its debts to Italianate gardening seem more deliberate—whether the format of regular central section bracketed with far less geometrical groves, the handsome pebblework and stone carving down the main axis, or the traditionally situated *giardino segreto*. While the eye is never trapped within the site, its opportunities for expansive and strongly associationist views are limited, so that the dialogue between enclosure and distance enjoyed at Le Balze is not resumed.

It is not merely our own hindsight that sees La Foce as a culmination of these other garden designs. Le Balze, I Tatti, and La Foce are so evidently examples of what T. S. Eliot sees as "a raid on the inarticulate"

> . . . every attempt
> Is a wholly new start, and a different kind of failure
> Because one has only learnt to get the better of words
> For the thing one no longer has to say, or the way in which
> One is no longer disposed to say it.[11]

And the lessons of each—vista versus enclosure, modernism versus tradition, personal representation versus generic garden formulae, the descent and ascent of terrace versus flatness of parterre, the play of hard-edge intervention versus the happenstance of natural growth, the play of larger landscape against immediate garden—are all pulled into a fresh and accomplished ensemble for Iris Origo. As the nine-year-old daughter of his patron, Lady Sybil Cutting, Iris must have watched Pinsent working at the Villa Medici from 1911; now, after the war they would have the opportunity to work together on a site that, while far less distinguished architecturally than Michelozzo's creation at Fiesole, would afford them the chance to make a distinguished modern landscape.[12]

If Pinsent brought to La Foce the same ideas or principles of design that he had used at these other sites, the circumstances of their application—new clients, a new site—would result in a very different garden. La Foce is a delight to the eye in every season, as Morna Livingston's photographs testify; it yields its design subtly and inexhaustibly to the most practiced eye of other designers (such as Laurie Olin) and to those who have lived there for many years, as Benedetta Origo has. It has elicited a series of short, celebratory essays, replete with beguiling imagery and bellettristic prose.[13] But it deserves a more thorough analysis, a way of explaining its magic and its workings, disclosing its "very disposition."[14] And I begin by asking precisely—following on Morna Livingston's photographic essay—what experiences of this garden and landscape are *not* visual, or, if visual to begin with, how are they translated into other modes. For if the full resources of human creativity and imagination are expended on making and maintaining fine gardens, as they have been at La Foce, then any account of them must also address a wide range of experience in gardens. While not ever denying, indeed always starting from, the palpable elements of La Foce, this essay tries to spell out what is not always at the surface of consciousness while we are in the gardens. For what may at first be something nonvisual in the garden and landscape becomes (as Laurie Olin has suggested) part of what we see as we get to know them better.

I have tried to chart some of the undercurrent of ideas and impressions that flow beneath Cecil Pinsent's design. In particular, this meant a "reading" of the gardens and landscape in the light of two exemplary books that Pinsent knew well: *On the Making of Gardens* by Sir George Sitwell, for whom Pinsent worked as architect on a small project, and the book dedicated to Pinsent by his architect friend, Geoffrey Scott, *The Architecture of Humanism*.[15]

As Benedetta Origo has explained, the landscape and gardens were established at La Foce after Antonio Origo and Iris Cutting purchased this derelict farmland and buildings prior to their marriage in 1924. As Antonio worked to subdue the barren territory, turning the bare clay hills—the *crete senesi*—into a productive and even georgic landscape, Iris and Pinsent created the gardens. These came in roughly four stages after the initial work to make the buildings habitable and their approaches rational: in 1927, the first garden, with its pool and arbor; in 1933, the lemon garden was started, as was the cemetery in the woods; in 1938, the rose garden and succeeding hillsides were brought into the ensemble; and in 1939, on the eve of war, the lower garden with its travertine grotto and encircling stairways was established. All the while, the larger agrarian landscape was being recovered, reshaped, and recolonized.

These gardens are marked by three exceptional qualities. First, they discover and make palpable for inhabitants and visitors the nature and meaning of the site where they are laid out; in other words, a *genius loci* is identified and drawn out. Second, Pinsent's design does so by establishing, deliberately and implicitly, a relationship between the inner gardens and the larger landscape beyond, work on both of which advanced simultaneously. Third, while wholly alert to the traditions of Italianate gardening and so to its role as a *lieu de mémoire*, it is splendidly, confidently modern; it makes—to quote Scott now for the first time—"past things contemporary with present [ones]."[16]

Once we are inside the gardens at La Foce we are made fully aware of their dialogue with the surrounding countryside. But long before we are inside looking out, this dialogue between the immediate garden and the larger landscape is initiated. Out in the countryside around La Foce, but especially from the west, its clusters of cypress gesture us toward some special place, some concentration of interest. We are alerted—or should be—before we actually arrive to the discovery of what the French call an *haut lieu*, a high or special place.

No garden exists independently of how we approach it—literally and topographically—though sometimes that relationship has been lost by subsequent interventions in its vicinity or by different uses of space. La Foce is a splendid instance of this, as Pinsent realized above all when he orchestrated our sense of arrival from the direction of Chianciano along the only road then open to motor vehicles. As they arrive, visitors bear left off the road and at once enter an amphitheatrical zone, with low curved walls marked by pillars with urns and polyhedronic stone balls on the right, and the taller gateway to the house on the left. Here the view is orientated toward the distant Val d'Orcia landscape, framed momentarily over another low wall bracketed by more pillars. Visitors cannot miss this vista straight ahead as their vehicle slows to make a ninety-degree turn up the short, cypress-lined driveway toward the original façade of the house.

This sequence of larger landscape, followed by the enclosed "formal" entry, then the building façade with its Peruzzi-like[17] rhythm of arches and windows and, eventually, progression through the interior would have led the original visitors into the gardens beyond. Today's less formal approach does not entirely lose this sense of context—the countryside is registered as the road climbs from Chianciano, that same calculated view across the Val d'Orcia is fleetingly implied before we enter alongside the buildings of the *fattoria,* and thence proceed through a small garden area into the house. That garden offers several routes, typical of less structured times: one ramp leads down to the cellar, while another, added in the 1970s by Enrico Gentiloni Silverj, leads upward under an arbor toward the house, which is also approached through an arch in the hedge and between an irregularly quartered garden; a third access, to the kitchen, leads across another garden of swiveled squares of hedge.

If I insist so much upon the approach, even before we have got into the gardens "proper," it is because the full impact of the latter is liable to repress the memory of our approach and how it had in fact shrewdly prepared us for subsequent experiences. Both Laurie Olin and I were compelled independently to revisit the approaches in order to work out in detail how Pinsent had programmed our first impressions even as we crossed the threshold of La Foce.[18] No visitor can recall in its fullness the rich history of that landscape presented upon arrival; the texture of its story, as Benedetta Origo has presented it here, is complex and only to be understood through study and meditation. Yet it is nonetheless a strong element of this site, part of its special quality; hence Pinsent's insistence in his original approach that the visitor register, however subliminally, its power and significance.

Entry from the house into the gardens is by contrast a subtle, even deliberately underplayed, event. As Benedetta Origo has described, Pinsent's first work in 1924 was to add two floors to the nineteenth-century southern extension of the original villa, but this still left the "main" exit from the villa via the big *salone* and into the oblong space or courtyard alongside the sixteenth-century building; from which garden, as it became, two low-key exits lead visitors into the larger garden spaces—one through an opening at the far right, the other up a ramp parallel with the side of the building and into the garden which nowadays is a guest's usual access. For only subsequently was the present entry from the kitchen wing given more prominence: what was at first only a flower room (*stanzino dei fiori*) became Benedetta's breakfast room in the 1990s and is now the usual entry into the garden, glimpsed first under a pergola with the fountain beyond; from here an opening in the hedge reveals a long axis through what will prove to be the main lemon garden.

The contrast between Pinsent's public or "formal" access, with its clear intimation of the relationship of villa site to Tuscan countryside, and the indirect, private, or "informal" means of reaching the garden through the interiors of the villa itself is part of the meaning of La Foce. Its agrarian world, so dear to the heart of Antonio and Iris Origo, so much the very foundation of early habitation there, was a distinct part of public, even political life, to which the buildings that Pinsent added in the landscape—the farmhouses or *case coloniche*,[19] the school buildings, the infirmary, the Dopolavoro[20]—all contributed. By contrast, the garden, though it would not refuse to look out over that same territory, was private, intimate, and correspondingly less immediately available. While its inhabitants could see out, its interior was suitably protected from outside by high retaining walls along the west and south of the site. Hence, perhaps, the shocking disruptions of the war, as narrated by Iris

Origo in her moving book *War in Val d'Orcia*, when the harsh realities of war intruded into the very spaces of the garden.

Long before the garden itself was established and before the surrounding agricultural land surrendered to all the activities that the La Foce photo albums record—*spietramento* (removal of stones from fields), plowing with oxen, drainage, regrading the slopes, digging artificial lakes, planting olive groves— the dream of an ambient landscape was crystallized in 1929 on the walls of the dining room. Here frescoes of ideal scenery imply a different world, in the tradition of other famous Italian interiors like those at the Villa Farnesina or at Palladio's villa at Maser. Amid these delicate fantasies the Origos always ate (only rarely *al fresco*, as our modern taste prefers). Perhaps with such strong imagery outside, these slight and fanciful *immagini* within were deemed sufficient. Yet, along with the estate map painted nearby on the staircase wall, they also serve to highlight a major theme of La Foce: the dialogue or *paragone* between real and ideal, natural and abstract, between what Geoffrey Scott variously termed "materials" and "poetry" or, alternatively, "the eye" and "the fancy,"[21] and—finally—between inside and outside.

Among the many visual delights of La Foce, the relation of inside to outside is striking. First, there is the relation of villa interior to garden exterior; then, of the different garden spaces—some more inward, enclosed, some opening out to involve the larger landscape; finally, of the gardens to the countryside that is constantly called to our attention as we explore the former. But the gradations of control or contrivance that sustain these "references" to an exterior world are not so easily captured in one static image, whether drawn or photographed. For, as we move, we carry with us hints or recollections of spaces passed through a moment ago.

The views out into the agrarian landscape are the most obvious and striking. As one walks down the central axis from the fountain garden, the long vista beckons; though just as one thinks it may open out at one's feet, like a similar "balcony" experience at the nearby Pienza palace garden,[22] we discover the lower grotto garden, which postpones the distant countryside for a space longer. Or, if we climb the terraces into the rose garden and from there either follow the pathway along the contour underneath the pergola or climb the cypress allée up the hillside, the view is always there, always framing the immediate garden experience.

The larger vistas are not, however, either homogenous or entirely what we would expect, even if we preserve sharp memories of our arrival across this landscape. To start with, of course, they change seasonally, as the rhythms and functions of the agricultural year dictate. Then, again, there is a distinct difference between the long view toward Monte Amiata and the shorter view across to the hillside that parallels the hillside pathway. The long view is as various as any cultural landscape could be: ruins, fields, villages (especially at night when lights betray their presence), lakes, hillsides, crags. Clearly, this is a landscape that bears the marks of centuries of cultivation, occupation, and movement, yet not a studied or fully composed landscape. That distinction belongs to the other conspicuous hillside, so distinctive in fact that it has itself become a postcard cliché, a Tuscany to send to friends back home even if you have never been to La Foce and seen it for yourself.

From the garden foreground, across fields and stands of trees down on the valley floor, you see a long hillside, green in spring, golden brown or dusty yellow by summer and autumn. Up this winds, in the form of two joined and backward Ss, a stony track edged with cypresses (once regularly spaced, their intervals are now somewhat irregular). The gesture is striking, and it stands out tellingly on that spur of hillside. Road and cypresses were planned by Antonio Origo when the hillside was recovered from the *creti*; Pinsent may have lent advice. A couple of farmhouses can be glimpsed toward the top of the bends that offer their inhabitants (and others whose houses are out of sight) one route down toward the *fattoria* at La Foce, the working hub of the whole estate. Practical exigency has been turned into a striking aesthetic gesture, yet an aestheticism that springs subtly from practical circumstance and tradition. For the road and its tell-tale cypress markers have perhaps another role to play—they tell of a farmed landscape so cared for, so enhanced, that it is nothing short of a garden itself: Tuscan countryside as designed landscape. If it recalls the wonderful, preternatural landscape through which the Three Magi travel in Benozzo Gozzoli's frescoes in the chapel of the Medici Palace in Florence (Pinsent's inspiration, even?), this is no accident: La Foce's zigzag relates modern agricultural successes to earlier myths of Tuscany's natural perfections.

To gaze at that soft-edged zigzag of track and trees from La Foce garden—indeed, surely, the best view of it, and meant to be—suggests one other aspect of the *genius loci* that Pinsent contrived or helped the Origos to draw out of the locality. Something apprehended instinctively, perhaps, it seems cumbersome when explained: it has to do with varying ratios of human control in different parts of the landscape.

As we walk from the house through the gardens, we might be aware, in the first place, of how stone plays against foliage, line and edge against blurred masses of leaf or flower, inorganic against organic, and vice versa, like the *aubretia campanula* erupting between the stonework as we descend to the lower garden. Then, we become gradually aware, especially as we move further from the house and climb up or along the hillside, how these contests between architectural control and natural (dis)order are not random. To start with, there is more distinct and palpable order the nearer we are to the building itself; further, the dialogue between hard and soft elements, between geometry and horticultural happenstance, between what is basically worked or carved stone and abundant plant material, is central to the experience of this garden (as of any garden, but potently so, when the design is as accomplished as Pinsent's).

We knew Pinsent was much taken with geometry, as we see at I Tatti and Le Balze. He was equally amused by Iris Cutting's inability to cope with it; in some verses appended to a drawing, he imagined the sixteen-year-old girl's despair at the subject:

Oh what's the use of circles, squares,
And all such dry Euclidian wares?

Lines, triangles and angles
Get mixed up in such awful tangles.
Oh! Only if I saw my way
To make such arid matter stay,
And leave an impress of some kind
On my sublime, Poetic mind!

That was in 1918; in the gardens he started making at La Foce for Iris after she married Antonio Origo in 1924, he found a way of melding geometry and sublime poetry. In more solemn fashion, his friend Geoffrey Scott had written that "however deeply Order and Proportion may characterise the laws of Nature, they are far to seek in its arrangement" and are often obscured in artistic creations by "an emphasis on . . . fidelity to the natural fact."[23] Yet before the onslaught of the picturesque that Scott so deprecated and Sir George Sitwell particularly denounced, what is often termed the "formal" garden had been particularly eloquent at drawing out the Order and Proportion that lurked in nature, yet without wholly suppressing a delight in "natural fact." As many mathematicians and designers had observed—Galileo, Christopher Wren, John Evelyn—the arts and science available to the garden designer were not to be deployed for their own sakes, but to draw out the secrets and delights of the natural world.

Pinsent's formal moves at La Foce are therefore less vocabulary than syntax, less a selection of effects than a series of linked moves.[24] His resourceful invocation of circles, lines, squares is to express his delight in the wondrous raw materials that a landscape architect is given. This shows, basically, in two ways. There are the endless variations on the theme of hard:soft as we move through the lemon terraces and down into the lower garden: plants cascading from urns, water held like glass in a stone basin, wisteria and roses escaping from their rigid pergolas, terra-cotta shapes alongside clipped hedges. Then as we move further from the house, climbing through the rose garden and up the hillside, or turning along the arbor walk that follows the curve of the hillside to the south, we realize that the artifice becomes less evident and insistent. Perhaps we notice it because we have responded instinctively to the play of forms in the gardens below. "Forms impose their own aesthetic character on a duly sensitive attention, quite independently of what we may know, or not know, about them."[25]

The contrasts within the lower gardens, though, are never stable. They change with the lights and shadows, or with seasons and patterns of growth. Take the clipped hedges, for example: vegetative, yet when recently clipped they ape walls that we find elsewhere in the gardens; but as the plants grow, the sharp edges gradually become fuzzy, slightly blurred, until the shears restore the wall-like effect once again.

It is a different matter with the contrasts that take place along pathways or sightlines leading out of the garden, eventually into the countryside. These are less fortuitous; indeed, Pinsent leads the garden visitor gradually from the order of urns, balustrades, shaped pools, arbors, clipped hedges, lemon pots, and mown grass to less dominant or insistent forms. As we climb the hillside, the steps are grass, though the risers are still in stone. The terracing follows the lines of the hill; once I saw them in the process of being mown, with the levels all close-cropped and the sides still in long grass—a fine gradation. The statue we find when we reach the summit bears a basket of fruit, a cornucopia of natural produce; whereas we may now recall that his pair in the lower garden (presumably they were once gate piers) is represented as a worker with a bundle of gardening tools on his back. Labor, art, horticulture in the garden; up here on the hill, the fruits of nature itself.

But the most subtle part of this scale or declension of the ratio art:nature occurs along the pathway that follows the side of the rose garden, and like a balcony overlooks the gardens below and gives the best views out across the countryside. Again, its subtlety is such that we probably barely register the effect as we follow along underneath its pergola. The views outward over the countryside and to that zigzag roadway on the opposite hill absorb all of our attention. So it is more likely to be on our return that we perceive, now in reverse, the changes in emphasis.

The path had eventually led into a wood, winding down to the Origo family cemetery and memorial chapel on the road below, of which more later. Returning through the wood and its wildflowers, the path emerges onto a grass platform; to our right, probably unnoticed on the way out, is a path that climbs to the hilltop and its cornucopia-bearing statue. Straight ahead is the path that will take us back to the house. The path is known as the *voltabotte* (barrel vault): wooden poles set in the ground support the iron pergola arches that begin there. On the upward hill side, these poles descend into a sloping bank the grass of which merges with the flagstones of the path; but its left or outward edge, toward the view, is molded with a ribbed stone. The path is straight enough, but soon bends outward, to the left, and immediately a low hedge rises on the left (into which the pergola poles now descend), while clumps of flowers begin to edge the hill side of the path. The path continues and then bends back to the right, still hugging the hill. At this juncture a bench is set against some cypresses in the hillside, an ideal belvedere from which the countryside can be surveyed; behind it a series of now almost buried exedras offers another ascent of the hill to the statue. But we stick to the path along the hill: now the rose garden begins on our right, the hedge on the left becomes a low wall, and the flagstones are now bounded by ribbed stone on both sides. There is one more bend, at which point the flags extend straight to the wall on our left to create a balcony effect that takes in the range of gardens below, somewhat obstructed by the growth of wisteria. Soon we reach the stone steps back into the lemon garden and see the roofs of the old stables and service buildings outside the garden wall; behind us the grass staircase leads up the cypress allée onto the hill.

From the wood's edge to the villa, the slow, gradual, incremental emphasis on stone, artifice, control, regimen has marked our steps. It was what Geoffrey Scott hailed as the "transition from house to landscape,"[26] though here we have followed it in reverse. And always to our left across the valley that zigzag road, clearly not just an agricultural route, picked out in cypress trees, nudges us to contemplate the intricate mediations of art and nature. "Every experience of art," wrote Scott, "contains, or may contain, two elements, the one direct, the other indirect. The direct element includes our sensuous experience and simple perceptions of form: the immediate apprehension of the work of art in its visible or audible material. . . . Secondly, and beyond this, there are the associations which the work awakens in the mind—our conscious reflections upon it, the significance we attach to it, the fancies it calls up, and which, in consequence, it is sometimes said to express."[27]

In the "necessary balance between formal and significant elements," La Foce achieves a rare equilibrium. Graphic and photographic imagery best celebrates its formal life. Words have to spell out the "significances," even though Geoffrey Scott warned that "a literary ideal . . . is never without menace to an art of form." Among the most insistent of these significances at La Foce are the memories of old Italian gardens, of which Sir George Sitwell had been such an ardent advocate. In this regard Pinsent would have listened to his friend Scott ("Italy seems but a pageant of great suggestions"),[28] to Iris Origo, brought up in the Villa Medici at Fiesole, and to the experience they all three must have had of villa gardens throughout Tuscany. Pinsent had himself worked at the Villa Medici and clearly enjoyed an intimate and extensive knowledge of Italianate garden art.

The hint of Gozzoli's Medici chapel frescoes in the zigzag, cypress-lined road is, however, the apt starting point for our inquiry. Perhaps an allusion, at most a quotation, it still takes its place in an agricultural landscape reclaimed and refashioned in modern times and by modern techniques. However much we may like to view the La Foce landscape and garden as ancient, full of the "ancestral memories" that Sitwell sought in old gardens, it is a creation of the 1920s and 1930s, albeit set within the Val d'Orcia, a cultural landscape of great antiquity. The Italian reminiscences in Pinsent's work, at La Foce as at Le Balze and I Tatti, are undeniably strong: it is through a knowledge of antecedents, as Scott put it, that new "things are [made] intelligible." Or again, historical elements "do a dual service by stimulating the sense of history while they set off the immaculate consistency of the [present] time."[29]

So many antecedents are quoted: shaped hedges, the arbors, the compartments of the lemon garden, the pergolas, the urns atop walls and balustrades, the grotto with stairs descending on either side, the baroque-inspired basin and fountains, the two sculptures (on the hill and in the lower garden). A miscellany of past garden events, not even—when old—from the same period. And when they are new, like the polyhedronic balls or the stone benches, the carving is simply modern, clear, machinelike (even if manually executed). If Pinsent learned the excitements of shaping space from Geoffrey Scott, he translated the latter's taste for baroque into a firmly modernist mode. The geometries above all are modern, like the shifted square within square of box hedges at the side entry (an echo of an earlier Pinsent design for the Villa Medici, Fiesole), or—more elaborately—the play with truncated triangles in the lower garden, perhaps borrowed from the Horti Leonini in San Quirico: the obelisks at the foot of the stairway echoed first in the horizontal forms of the box compartments and then in the tapered shape of the whole lower garden itself.[30] These tangible gestures of today are crowned by the insertion of *magnolia grandiflora* in the center of the hedged compartments—a wholly unhistorical device, yet a calculated salute to an Anglo-American patron and typical of horticultural taste at that time.

For the daughters of Antonio and Iris Origo, Benedetta and Donata, La Foce is full, naturally, of memories. For others, these memories may be, in part, contrived by the disposition of the place; or they will be, partly, accidental. Those, for instance, who have read Iris Origo's writings, especially *War in Val d'Orcia*, but also *Images and Shadows*, will find this territory full of recollections.[31] But if the gardens and landscape do not afford other visitors such an immediate release of associations, they might do worse than go to the cemetery that Cecil Pinsent designed for the family and the community. For, to start with, cemeteries are essentially places of memory.

It is reached either by the road that passes along the hillside below the garden wall and continues toward Chiarentana or by taking the pathway alongside the rose garden and then through the woodland, looping down to the side of the tiny *campo santo* enclosure.[32]

Pinsent's acute acknowledgment of historical precedence—Alberti and Peruzzi generally, the Pazzi Chapel in particular—blends with his astonishing sensitivity to present circumstance. Designed originally for the burial of Gianni Origo, who died at the age of seven in 1933, the graveyard has filled over the years with the graves of his parents, Antonio and Iris, of local folk who worked for them, and of soldiers who died in the war. It is in itself a record of La Foce, above all for those who can read between the lines of its graves and their inscriptions. Because it is situated beyond the gardens yet is linked to them by the path through the woods as well as by its deliberate planting (a sudden, ordered florescence in the woodland), it announces itself as the culmination of a journey, even for the living who can turn away and retrace their steps. It is as shapely as anything in the gardens: rows of markers, the formal geometry of its space (a rectangle broken by the intrusion on one side of the oblong chapel). Yet a final surprise awaits us within this ordered and mortuary world: as we turn away from the Palladian façade of the chapel, always open, and walk down the central pathway toward the gateway, with the resting places of the dead on either side, what we see through the open ironwork is a huge and wondrous live oak tree.

NOTES

1. Letter to Bernard Berenson, in the archives at Villa I Tatti.

2. Papers on this theme of the relationships of gardens to landscapes were presented at a symposium at the Isabella Stewart Gardner Museum, Boston, and the collection was published as a special issue of *Studies in the History of Gardens and Designed Landscapes* 19 (1999).

3. François Jullien, *The Propensity of Things: Towards a History of Efficacy in China*, trans. Janet Lloyd (New York, 1995). This extraordinary study has much to offer the analysis of garden art, western as well as eastern, though it touches but rarely upon it. By accident I started reading this while on a visit to La Foce, so it is perhaps inevitable that it has become entangled in my thinking about the place. I am grateful to both Geoffrey Lloyd and Stanislaus Fung for independently drawing my attention to Jullien's work.

4. The literature on Pinsent's career consists mainly of the collection of essays, *Cecil Pinsent and His Gardens in Tuscany*, ed. Marcello Fantoni, Heidi Flores, and John Pfordresher (Florence, 1996); there is also Ethne Clarke's "A Biography of Cecil Ross Pinsent, 1884–1963," *Garden History* 28 (1998), 176–91. See also Erica Neubauer, "The Garden Architecture of Cecil Pinsent 1884–1964 [*sic*]," *Journal of Garden History* 3 (1983), 35–48; David Ottewill, *The Edwardian Garden* (New Haven and London, 1989), 159–63; and Richard M. Dunn, *Geoffrey Scott and the Berenson Circle* (Lampeter, 1998).

5. It is interesting to note that two innovative garden designers, Reginald Blomfield and C. F. A. Voysey, were on the staff of the Architectural Association during Pinsent's time there (see Dunn, *Geoffrey Scott*, 52, and Ottewill, *The Edwardian Garden*, for their work).

6. I borrow Clarke's formulation, "A Biography of Cecil Ross Pinsent," 183.

7. Pinsent's and Geoffrey Scott's sketches of this narrow site are reproduced by Neubauer, "The Garden Architecture of Cecil Pinsent," figures 7–9.

8. Clarke has also suggested that this introspective aspect of the gardens reflected the personality of their owner, since Strong was something of a philosopher manqué, "A Biography of Cecil Ross Pinsent," 183.

9. These are illustrated in the small book by Daniela Mignani, *The Medicean Villas by Giusto Utens* (Florence, 1991).

10. Pinsent apparently thought it could have been designed with more width: see Clarke, "A Biography of Cecil Ross Pinsent," 189. See also William Weaver, *A Legacy of Excellence: The Story of Villa I Tatti* (New York, 1997) for a fuller presentation of this garden than can be attempted in the context of this book.

11. T. S. Eliot, "East Coker," part V, *The Complete Poems and Plays, 1909–1950* (New York, 1958).

12. See James S. Ackerman, *The Villa* (Princeton, 1996).

13. These include C. Quest-Ritson, *The English Garden Abroad* (New York, 1992), mainly 128–31; Penelope Hobhouse, "Classical Interlude," *Gardens Illustrated* 37 (1998), 54–61; William Weaver, "Remembering Iris Origo in Tuscany," *Architectural Digest* (April 1991), 58, 62, 66; Patrick Rowe, "Designs on Tuscan Soil," *Country Life* (5 July 1990), 90–95; Marella Agnelli, *Gardens of the Italian Villas* (New York, 1987), 212–15.

14. Jullien, *The Propensity of Things*, 12.

15. Sitwell's volume was first published in London in 1909; my references are to that edition. It is also available in other editions, including Sacheverell, Osbert, Sir George, and Reresby Sitwell, *Hortus Sitwellianus* (Wilton, Salisbury, 1984). Scott's study, *The Architecture of Humanism*, first

appeared in London in 1914; a revised second edition was published in 1924. I have used the paperback edition of the latter (New York, 1956), but there are also recent editions, with an introduction by David Watkin (London, 1980) and with an introduction by Paul Barolsky (New York, 1999). The quotation used in the title of this essay is taken from Geoffrey Scott's book.

16. Scott, *The Architecture of Humanism,* 127. In this connection see also Pinsent's article "Giardini moderni all'italiana" in *Il Giardino Fiorito* 5 (June 1931), 69–73.

17. There is some general consensus, unconfirmed at present from any archival sources, that Baldassare Peruzzi (1481–1536) may have been responsible for the original building; he worked in and around Siena after fleeing from the Sack of Rome in 1527.

18. See his drawings of this feature: to avoid an excessive apparatus of cross-references, the reader is encouraged to move to and fro from this essay and Olin's drawings in this volume.

19. For the *case coloniche,* Pinsent provided only the basic architectural model; practical circumstances determined their location. But it seems unlikely that Pinsent did not at the very least discuss with Antonio Origo the placement of these items in the total landscape—siting was, after all, a major concern of both himself and Geoffrey Scott. La Foce was also the first commission for Pinsent where public and private aspects of the patron had to be represented.

20. *Dopolavoro* was a fascist term, signaling new concepts of agrarian community; we might call it now a community hall. On this larger theme of Tuscan agrarian life, see Emilio Sereni, *Storia del Paesaggio Agrario Italiano* (Bari, 1981), the works cited by Benedetta Origo in her essay above, and Jeff Pratt, *The Rationality of Rural Life: Economic and Cultural Change in Tuscany* (Chur, 1994).

21. Scott, *The Architecture of Humanism*, respectively 49 and 70.

22. The palace garden at Pienza cannot be an original Renaissance one, though the space certainly is; one wonders whether its modern reformulation may owe something to Pinsent's imaginative grasp of garden art, old and new. The dramatic presentation of the Tuscan countryside through the arches of the Pienza garden was an inevitable model for connecting an immediate garden space with a larger landscape.

23. Scott, *The Architecture of Humanism*, 69.

24. Cf. "On the one hand there is the disposition of things—their condition, configuration, and structure. On the other hand there is force and movement. The statis versus the dynamic. But this dichotomy, like all dichotomies, is abstract. It is a temporary means for the mind to represent reality, one that simplifies as it illuminates": Jullien, *The Propensity of Things,* 11.

25. Scott, *The Architecture of Humanism*, 93.

26. Ibid., 60.

27. Ibid., 55.

28. Respectively, in this paragraph ibid., 64, 138, and 27.

29. Ibid., respectively, 129 and 46.

30. Benedetta Origo has suggested, among other helpful comments on earlier drafts of this essay, that the rough-hewn obelisks are quoted from Piranesi.

31. Published in 1970, only the last part of *Images and Shadows* concerns La Foce. Earlier sections, though, are suggestive of the social and spatial worlds of country houses in Ireland, England, and America, the world out of which Iris drew her inspiration for La Foce. Iris's Anglo-Irish grandparents, for instance, lived at Desart Court, with its "Italian" garden (p. 40), its "park so green, the woods so deep in bluebells" (p. 57), all elements of a "garden and landscape" that

Pinsent worked with her to create at La Foce. And *Images and Shadows* also records her father's wish to make her a true internationalist—"Bring her up somewhere where she does not belong . . . so that she can really be cosmopolitan, deep down" (p. 88); this suggests some of the motivation as well as the tonal quality of La Foce—Italianate, yet conceived in a truly modern and large sense. Pinsent himself, it seems fairly certain, saw his work as inventing modern versions of an Italian *locus amoenus* rather than what Richard Dunn terms too straightforwardly "designing a Renaissance garden" (*Geoffrey Scott,* 81 and 85).

32. In Rome during January 1919 Pinsent wrote a poem, "Watteau," in which he prophetically announced this cemetery garden: "I know a garden, sheltered in a wood,/ Or wood, or garden, it was hard to say,—/ For in the midst a fluted temple stood . . ." Several of Pinsent's surviving verses, in scrapbooks at La Foce, treat of gardens, of the siting of buildings, or the "condition of music" (in the words of Walter Pater reiterated by Sir George Sitwell), to which such garden creations aspire.

MAPS

Rapolano

VAL DI CHIANA

Montepulciano

Pienza

Monticchiello

Montalcino

San Quirico
d'Orcia

Chianciano
Terme

Vignoni

Poccie Lattaie

Cava di Travertino

Spedaletto

Castelluccio
Dopolavoro

Lucciola Bella

Bagno Vignoni

VAL D'ORCIA

Ambulatorio Gianni Origo

Necropolis of Tolle
La Foce
Cemetery

Ripa d'Orcia
Rocca
d'Orcia

Via Cassia (s.s.2)

Crete
Zig-zag
road

Casa
dei
Bambini

Chiarentana

Chiusi

Castiglione
d'Orcia

Lake

Torre
Tarugi

River Orcia

Santa Maria
in Belverde

Eremo del Vivo

Vivo
d'Orcia

MONTE
CETONA

Orvieto

Bagni
di
San Filippo

Radicofani

Arcidosso

Abbadia
San Salvatore

MONTE
AMIATA

San Casciano
dei Bagni

0   1   2 Miles

0   1   2 Kilometers

Southern Tuscany

MAPS

298

Montepulciano

Chianciano
Terme

Castelluccio

Dopolavoro

Ambulatorio Gianni Origo
Casa dei Bambini
La Foce

Chiarentana

River Orcia

0   1/2   1 Mile

0   1/2   1 Kilometer

La Foce Estate

Notes on the Authors

BENEDETTA ORIGO runs the country property of La Foce, which her parents, Antonio and Iris Origo, created. A musician by training (the Florence Musical Conservatory), she also worked in publishing as a partner in Edizioni dell'Elefante, Rome, which issued several exhibition catalogues for the Houghton Library, Harvard University, for the Vatican Library, and for the Bibliotheca Herziana, also in Rome. She also translated works for publication there. With her cellist son, Antonio Lysy, she organizes a summer chamber music festival at La Foce (Incontri in Terra di Siena), as well as contemporary art exhibitions, garden courses, seminars on design, documentary films, and other cultural activities.

MORNA LIVINGSTON is a documentary photographer specializing in traditional buildings and landscapes. Born in New York, she lives in a colonial house in Old City, Philadelphia, and teaches design, drawing, and vernacular architecture in the School of Architecture and Design of Philadelphia University. She has traveled extensively to research and photograph buildings around the world. She is currently completing a book on medieval Indian water buildings to be published by Princeton Architectural Press and has received grants from the American Institute of Indian Studies, the Fulbright Association, and the Prince Charitable Trusts.

LAURIE OLIN is Practice Professor of Landscape Architecture at the University of Pennsylvania. His book *Across the Open Field: Essays Drawn from English Landscapes* was published by the University of Pennsylvania Press in 1999. A distinguished landscape architect and a Principal of Olin Partnership, Philadelphia, he has worked on projects at Bryant Park and Battery Park City, New York, and the Getty Center Gardens, Los Angeles. He has also published many essays on the history and theory of his profession, for which he was awarded the Bradford Williams Medal in 1991. He is a Fellow of the American Academy of Arts and Sciences and an Honorary Member of the American Institute of Architects.

JOHN DIXON HUNT is Professor of Landscape Architecture at the University of Pennsylvania and editor of the journal *Studies in the History of Gardens*. He has published widely on garden history and landscape theory, including editing *The Oxford Book of Garden Verse* (1993); most recently he has written *Greater Perfections: The Practice of Garden Theory* (University of Pennsylvania Press, 2000) and *The Picturesque Garden in Europe* (Thames & Hudson, 2001). He has traveled and researched extensively in Italy, having published *Garden and Grove: The Italian Renaissance Garden in the English Imagination, 1600–1750* in 1986 (reissued in paperback by the University of Pennsylvania Press in 1998). He is currently finishing a study of gardens in the city of Venice.